Tran

Joseph DeGraft-Amanfu

*All quotations are from the King James Version unless stated otherwise.

In this book, the term 'man,' represents male and female in most cases.

Also by Joseph DeGraft-Amanfu:

A Second Chance: ISBN 978-1-6064352-6-7

And coming soon:

Whom do men say that I am?: ISBN 978-0-60725-819-3

Dedication

I dedicate this book to God's children all over the world. The contents reveal what is considered normal for every Christian; it is about what each individual Christian possesses already. It is not the height of a believer's life or walk with God, but the beginning. Remember, ours is a high calling; it is a heavenly call. Besides your bible, which of course, should be your primary book, Transcended Life is the book that every Christian must have as a companion.

Even though this book is written specifically for Christians, I truly believe that anyone who wants to know what it takes to live as a Christian will also find this book the most enlightening.

Many thanks

To my dearest friend and Lord, (Holy Spirit) I give thanks and worship. May the name of our Lord and Savior Jesus Christ forever be praised and glorified.

My most heartfelt thanks to my dear wife, Miranda, and my precious children for standing with me and helping in so many ways to prepare this book.

I am particularly grateful to chief Editor Stephen Bess and Editors, Jan Montoya and Nomvuyo Qubeka for editing and getting this book ready for the press. May the blessings of the Lord be upon all who read this book, Amen.

Contents

MISSION

"Till we all come in the unity of the faith, and of the knowledge of the Son of God, unto a perfect man, unto the measure of the stature of the fullness of Christ: That we henceforth be no more children, tossed to and fro, and carried about with every wind of doctrine, by the sleight of men, and cunning craftiness, whereby they lie in wait to deceive; but speaking the truth in love, may grow up into him in all things, which is the head, even Christ" (Ephesians 4:13-15).

Chapter One

INTRODUCTION

 Transcended life is the life of a Christian. It is the resurrected or the new life of all those who have experienced rebirth; those who are indwelt, and led by God. If the birth of the God-Man (Jesus Christ) was a miracle of all miracles, then the birth of a Christian is a miracle. Christian is the name given to the disciples or followers of Christ. This name was first used in Antioch (Acts 11:26; 26:28; 1 Peter 4:16). Christians are no ordinary individuals or human beings, for they live in two realms: the spiritual and the natural. They are in the world, but not of the world. They are pilgrims and strangers in this world. Born of God, they are born again into this world as ambassadors for Christ.

The quality of the Christian life is transcended because it is the life of the indwelling Son of God, who lives His life in and through the new man; it is the life of the transcended Son of God reproduced and lived fully in the Holy Spirit: "He that is joined unto the Lord is one spirit" (1 Corinthians 6:17). Jesus Christ is not only the Life within the life of the Christian, but the Mind within the mind. The path of the Christian life is symbolic of the "Path which no fowl knoweth, and which the vulture's eye hath not seen" (Job 28:7); it is the mysterious life of all those who are born twice in this life, and as a result, possess two birth certificates with two dates of birth.

The phenomenon of the Christian life is that every Christian died one time with Christ and rose with Him; therefore, they are alive forever. Even though they may have to put off the old mortal body, no Christian shall ever die (John 11:26). Every Christian has already passed from death unto life. The new life is hid with God in Christ, beyond the destructive reach of any creature, even death (John 5:24).

For Christians, there is no difference between the realm of the natural and the supernatural because they live and work in both. Even though Christians like everybody else live in a natural body, they possess the capability to see visions, receive intimations, dream realities and manifest supernatural capabilities through the gifts of the Spirit. Through the gifts of the Holy Spirit, a Christian can see far beyond the realm of the natural. The invisible is as real as the visible because God made both; to the believing Christian, all things are possible.

Christians are victorious people; they are more than conquerors through Christ who strengthens them. Whether in battle with men, angels or demons from the pit of hell, in all things they stand undefeated for with them is an invincible force. Although Christians may sometimes appear materially poor or destitute, no man can underestimate them, for the poorest among them may be very rich before God. For them; "Godliness with contentment is a great gain" (1 Timothy 6:6; 3 John 2).

Every Christian is a free man irrespective of existing natural states or conditions; they may be incarcerated or in slavery but no matter what the state of their natural existence, they are free people. Through rebirth Christians are forever free in Christ. Even though Christians are law abiding, they are not subject to any human law per se. For them, any law that is in conflict with the Creator's will is not acceptable. Being freed and therefore free, they are bondservants of Jesus Christ.

Every Christian has only one goal and one concern in life, and that is to be like Jesus Christ; to be like Him in moral purity, power and faith; to be like Him by living a life that is pleasing to the Lord God. A common denominator for all Christians is that they hate every falsehood, evil scheme, and idea of wicked men, and it is this which separates them from the rest of the world. For example, no Christian can stand policies and laws that seek to take away the dignity, worth, and the humanity of mankind. Personal suffering for a Christian can be a rare opportunity and privilege to share in the suffering for the name of Jesus Christ.

Chosen by God for a special purpose, the daily duty of every Christian is to show forth the praises of Him who died to redeem mankind from all iniquity and bondage. Christians recognize no human classifications whatsoever: "There is neither Jew nor Greek, there is neither bond nor free, there is neither male nor female: for ye are all one in Christ Jesus" (Galatians 3:28). They see each other as belonging to one another, members of one body, one Lord, one hope of calling, one baptism, and one God and Father of all (Ephesians 4:3-6).

The invitation to be a Christian goes out to everybody, for every man is invited to be a partaker of the divine nature; to be a member of God's very own family. The agonizing part is that not everybody would accept God's offer. In fact, anybody can be a Christian; unfortunately, not everyone would be a Christian. There is only one way to enjoy transcended life and that is to be born and indwelt by God (1 Peter 1:16).

As a Christian, I write this book not as someone who has already attained perfection, but like some I seek that: "I may apprehend that for which also I am apprehended of Christ Jesus" (Philippians 3:12). My prayer for anyone who reads this book is that God would make available to you the riches of His glory, and that you will be strengthened with might by his Spirit in the inner man – that Christ may dwell in your heart by faith. That ye, being rooted and grounded in love, "may be able to comprehend with all saints what is the breadth, and length, and depth, and height; and to know the love of Christ, which passeth knowledge; that ye might be filled with all the fullness of God" (Ephesians 3:18-19).

Now, let me walk you through step by step all that makes the Christian life transcended, what it means to be a Christian and what it takes to remain a Christian. Further, we shall examine the different phases and the magnificent developments that make ordinary people transcended or supernatural; the mystery of a sinner becoming a saint, and why victory in life and service for a Christian is a settled matter. "What manner of man is this, that even the wind and the sea obey him?" Can also be said of a Christian who is led by the Holy Spirit (Mark 4:41).

Now unto him that is able to do exceeding abundantly above all that we ask or think, according to the power that worketh in us, make all His grace abound towards you as you prayerfully make your way through the pages of this book. Amen.

Chapter Two

Born of the Spirit

To be a Christian, you must be born again; you must experience a new birth; you must be born spiritually the second time. There are no other ways to becoming a Christian other than to be born of God; born from above, and by the imperishable Word of the Living God:

> **"Being born again, not of corruptible seed, but of incorruptible, by the word of God, which liveth and abideth forever" (1 Peter 1:23; 1John 3:9).**

We are living in a time and age in which every supernatural event is viewed with suspicion and skepticism, but to be candid, the birth of a Christian is a supernatural event. This is not a second natural birth, but a being begotten from above by the Holy Spirit:

> **"Verily, verily, I say unto thee, except a man be born of water and of the Spirit, he cannot enter into the kingdom of God' (John 3:5).**

If the birth of Jesus Christ was a miracle, then the birth of a Christian is also a miracle. Jesus Christ, in His incarnation, added to His divine nature the human nature; Christians, at new birth, add to their human nature, the divine nature. I can comfortably say that the creation of the new man is the second wonder in God's creation. The first is the creation of natural man (unregenerate man).

New birth is a necessity for every human being, because man who was made upright has become corrupt, depraved, and is perishing. Man's nature has become defiled (Ecclesiastes 7:29); his nature has become stained with sin and needs a new nature. The Second birth is the only means by which man is given a new nature. If any man wishes to have meaningful fellowship and communion with God, his maker, then he must be born again.

Further, because of sin, the image and likeness of God upon man has become defaced, and the new birth is the only way to give man a fresh start and a clean slate. Man, in his current state of derailment and estrangement is of no use to His maker and not even to himself.

It is absolutely impossible for unregenerate man to fulfill the purpose for which he is created without a new birth: "For we are His workmanship, created in Christ Jesus unto good works, which God hath before ordained that we should walk in them" (Ephesians 2:10). Man without a second birth cannot be good, and neither can he do good works. Every man must be born again and indwelt by the good God to do good works. Natural born man cannot be good, and neither can he do works; good is greatness, pure, and moral uprightness (Mark 10:18).

New birth or regeneration is solely a divine prerogative. It is exclusively the work of the Holy Spirit. It does not come by the natural desire for children, and neither is it the result of human decision; it is what God alone must begin and finish (Philippians 1:6). Salvation from start to finish is all of God. What God begins, He must finish (1 Samuel 3:12). Only the Creator of mankind can recreate or give man a second birth. No man can give himself a new birth; it must be done supernaturally by the omnipotent God:

"Which were born, not of blood, nor of the will of the flesh, nor of the will of man, but of God" (John 1:13).

Transcended life, which is life in Christ, begins with birth in the Spirit; it begins with the birth of the New Man. Born of the Spirit, every Christian is considered a spirit being. Our newly created spirit is one with the Holy Spirit: "But he that is joined unto the Lord is one spirit (1 Corinthians 6:17). This means oneness with the Spirit. This means man can effectively commune with God, through the Holy Spirit. Spirituality begins at birth by the Holy Spirit.

Only the Spirit of God can produce that which is spiritual and holy. The birth of a saint is a divine prerogative; no man can make himself a saint and neither can any man confer sainthood on another. Every born again is a Christian, and every Christian is a saint:

"And that ye put on the new man, which after God is created in righteousness and true holiness" (Ephesians 4:24).

Spirit gives birth to spirit and the flesh gives birth to flesh and the two are mutually exclusive. For example, after the fall of man and after the death of the first two sons of Adam, Cain and Abel, Adam lived a hundred and thirty years, and begat a son in his own likeness, and image, and called his name Seth (Genesis 5:3). Adam was created in the likeness and image of God (verse 2), but Seth was born after the likeness and image of Adam, which means Seth was born after the corrupt nature of Adam, and not after Adam as he was originally made from the hands of his maker.

Like Seth, each of us through the process of natural birth hath received from Adam through our parents a sinful, corrupt, and defiled nature (cf. Romans 5). Every man has inherited from Adam what became of them after his fall; therefore every man must be born again. Fleshly born, every man must be Spirit born; procreation must give way to regeneration. Man born of the flesh cannot please God; therefore, new birth is indispensable:

"That which is born of the flesh is flesh; and that which is born of the Spirit is spirit" (John 3:6).

God does not waste His time to improve, repair, or reform the old nature at regeneration. God creates a completely new man. God gives to every one of His newly born a completely new nature; a divine nature. As a result, every Christian possesses two natures: human and divine nature — but beware, that the second birth is not reincarnation. Christianity has no room for something absurd such as reincarnation.

Man, as created by God, can only be born twice: The natural birth, by which every man enters the world, and the Spiritual birth which saves sinners and translates them into the kingdom of Christ and of God, and making them members of God's own family.

Our human nature (what we are as human beings without a second birth) can only adapt us for natural existence. Our divine nature (what we are as a result of rebirth) adapts us for spiritual existence which is life in the Spirit or heavenly existence. In God's creation everything has its proper place:

"If there is a natural body, there is also a spiritual body" (1 Corinthians 15:44).

Christian life is very unique because every Christian possesses two dates of birth with two birth certificates; one certificate from the place of birth and the other, from above. Besides the natural birthday, Christians can also celebrate a second spiritual birthday which is the day we became born again.

I must emphasize, one birth is not good enough to qualify anyone for the blissful life promised to all those who put their faith in God. There is no other way to become a Christian than to be born again by the Spirit of God. Christians become partakers of God's very own nature at regeneration (2 Peter 1:4):

"Jesus answered and said unto him, Verily, verily, I say unto thee, except a man be born again, he cannot see the kingdom of God" (John 3:3).

_____

"But as many as received him, to them gave he power to become the sons of God, even to them that believe on his name" (John 1:12).

Every Christian is a new creation by virtue of the new birth (2 Corinthians 5:17). To be in Christ is to be a new creation; everyone who is born of God is a new creation and not that he ought to be a new creation. He is a new man, even though he remains in the same old mortal frame (body).

A Christian is a new man in an old suit; he is white, not whitewashed. The old life of slavery to sin and bondage to Satan is a thing of the past; behold, everything has become new. There is a decisive break with the old life at the moment of salvation. Regeneration is a divine transformation. It is a gift from God, and signifies a new beginning.

New birth is irreversible; it cannot be repeated. What God does is forever. A man can repent or be converted many times but not so with regeneration. Like the natural birth, it is absurd to think of the possibility of becoming unborn. The difference between natural life and the Spiritual life in Christ, is so striking: Sinners become saints and old men become new men. New man is God's masterpiece (Ephesians 2:1,10; Colossians 3:10).

The transcendent nature of the new birth is that all three persons of the Godhead are involved in the making. God gave mankind salvation, Jesus bought it, and the Holy Spirit brought it to us:

"Not by works of righteousness which we have done, but according to his mercy he saved us, by the washing of regeneration, and renewing of the Holy Ghost" (Titus 3:5).

"You have he (God) quickened, who were dead in trespasses and sins, hath quickened us together with Christ, (by grace are you saved)" (Ephesians 2:1ff).

Jesus "gave himself for us, that he might redeem us from all iniquity, and purify unto himself a peculiar people, zealous of good works" (Titus 2:14).

Good deeds, rich heritage, education, good morals, and sound religion may be good, but unfortunately, they fall far too short of producing such a transcended birth — the birth of a new man. Further, new birth is not in the human gene and neither is it an inner divine spark that each of us can ignite to produce a new man.

Further still, reformation, renovation, or repair may produce some positive changes in a person, but not a new man. Self-effort cannot provide salvation and neither can it emancipate fallen man from the tentacles of sin and death. Salvation has nothing to do with merits; no man can earn his salvation and neither can it be awarded:

God alone chooses and determines the rebirth of each of His sons.

Now, let me show you another mystery of the Christian life. Even though Christian life begins at rebirth as already mentioned, realistically, the idea began with God from eternity past; it began in the dateless past, before history:

"Who hath saved us, and called us with a holy calling, not according to our works, but according to his own purpose and grace, which was given us in Christ before the world begun,

But is now made manifest by the appearing of our Savior Jesus Christ, who hath abolished death, and hath brought life and immortality through the gospel" (2 Timothy 1:9).

The choice of individual Christians were made before each individual was born from the mother's womb, and before salvation. Each individual Christian was chosen according to God's own eternal purpose before birth (cf. Galatians 1:15):

"According as he hath chosen us in him before the foundation of the world, that we should be holy and without blame before him in love" (Ephesians 1:4).

However beware, for this does not imply God had destined or chosen certain individuals for hell; it always has been and still is the will of God that all men be saved, that no man should perish (1 Timothy 2:4). Ephesians 1:4 simply means the omniscient God, by His foreknowledge, chose and made provisions according to His own purpose and grace for all who are to be saved before history, but we are only made aware of it by the appearing of our Savior Jesus Christ through faith in history (cf. Acts 2:47).

I wish I can tell you what is in God's foreknowledge that determined His choice of people but since no man is privileged to know, we can only rejoice in our unique privilege and be forever grateful to God for choosing us. The all-knowing God had a plan for the salvation of mankind long before the fall of man; and before sin was introduced into the world by Satan.

God has a plan and a purpose for creating mankind and nothing can by any means destroy or abort His purpose, not even sin. God's plan has a determinate end for all those who are chosen and called. Each individual would be made exactly like His Son Jesus Christ, that is, in righteousness and true holiness forever. Jesus Christ is the express image of God, and the brightness of His glory; He is the visible form of the invisible God. Christians resemble God in holiness and righteousness (Romans 8:28-30).

God's redemption plan has three stages: He first calls all those whom He had chosen individually through the Gospel of His Son Jesus Christ. He then justifies, and sanctifies them by his word and the Spirit, and He would finally glorify them at the second appearance of His Son:

"Moreover whom he did predestinate, them he also
called: and whom he called, them he also justified: and
whom he justified, them he also glorified" (Romans
8:30; cf. 1:6; 3:24, 28, 4:2; 5:1; 8:17; Colossians 1:27;
3:4; Titus 2:13-15).

There are many benefits to the new birth with great
privileges and promises. For example, everyone born of the
Spirit is automatically given by grace, a new standing before
the Holy God; he is declared righteous (justified) on the merits
of Jesus Christ through faith. His righteousness is imputed to
each and every Christian through faith.

Faith in the faith of Jesus Christ is reckoned as righteousness
to every believer (Romans 3:22). In other words, God credits or
puts into the accounts of each of His saints all that Jesus is and
did for them:

"But of him are ye in Christ Jesus, who of God is made
unto us wisdom, and righteousness, and sanctification,
and redemption" (1 Corinthians 1:30).

Again, to each individual Christian, there is righteousness
imparted; born again is a state. There is the impartation of
righteousness:

"I will give you a new heart and put a new spirit in you; I
will remove from you your heart of stone and give you a
heart of flesh" (Ezekiel 36:26).

At rebirth, every Christian is given a new heart and a new
spirit and is washed clean by the word of God. Every Christian
is sanctified by the word and by the Spirit. There are many other
benefits including the reconciliation of Jews and Gentles, who
both have peace and access to God through Christ Jesus. I hope
to give you the summary of a few at the end of this chapter and
also cover more in the chapters ahead, but for now let me give
you a little homework to do; ponder over Ephesians 2:11-22.

Born of the Spirit is the starting point for union and
communion with God for every man. Fortunately, there is

nothing like a counterfeit or false Christian. It is a question of being a Christian or not, new or old, white or white washed. As already mentioned, new or white is what God is looking for, in every man or creature, and this can only come about through divine transformation.

New life is free for all who express the need for it; it is free for all who come to God through the Faith of His Son Jesus Christ. All those who are born again are marked to be glorified at a date in history (1 Corinthians 15:49-58); creation shall also be reformed on the day of Christ (Romans 8:18-22).

Beloved, I have no doubt you picked this book because God has chosen you for this transcended life through His beloved Son Jesus Christ. However, if at this moment, you are not certain, or sure of your salvation, then, you may be missing out on this supernatural and exciting Christian journey.

Satan is a thief and a murderer who seeks to take advantage of the weak and the ignorant. For the benefit of the doubt and for your sake, let me quickly show you how you can solidify your stand as a Christian and forever cast away the spirit of unbelief, fear and doubt, so that you can enjoy the rest of this book.

Before we begin, be aware that the process or the way to becoming born again is very simple and straightforward. God has done all the difficult part through His Son Jesus Christ. What you are getting is a finished product. Your part is to listen, believe and receive. Symbolically, look at it this way— God through His Son has cooked the food, set the table and is inviting you to come and dine with Him. One spiritual birth is all you need and your salvation is secured forever.

Know that, every man must will his entrance into the new life that God is offering to mankind through Christ (Mark 9:45; John 7:17; 1 Timothy 2:4). We must all will our salvation or damnation. God has given to each and every human being an equal opportunity to choose life in Christ or death in sin (1 Timothy 2:3-6). Sinful man cannot save himself; man has gotten himself too dirty to make himself clean and too deep to

get himself out. Sin is cancerous and only fools make mockery
of it. Heaven is open to all, even though not everyone may want
to be in heaven.

How to be Saved

No differences exist among human beings and human need.
The wages of sin is death for every man. Likewise, the gift of
God is eternal life through Jesus Christ and free for all who
choose to believe (Romans 6:23):

> **"For God so loved the world, that he gave his only begot-
> ten Son, that whosoever believeth in him should not per-
> ish, but have everlasting life. For God sent not his Son
> into the world to condemn the world; but that the world
> through him might be saved" (John 3:16-17).**

The standard by which every man is judged is the
righteousness of Jesus Christ, and by that, every man born into
this world must be born again or face the wrath of God. Because
humanity has sinned against God, it is no longer up to man to
determine his own destiny. Every man must count on the grace
and mercy of God for his redemption. Salvation for sin ridden
man depends entirely on the grace of God: "For the wages of sin
is death" (Romans 6:21).

Sin taking a back seat in every man or dwelling in the flesh
is the reason flesh and blood (natural born) cannot enter into
the Kingdom, for it is impossible for man not to sin (John 8:44).
The two men, Jesus and Adam, stand for death or life for every
man:

> **"For as in Adam all die, even so in Christ shall all be
> made alive" (1 Corinthians 15:22).**

Despite man's hopelessness and helplessness there is good
news for every man by the grace and mercy of God. What
God has done for every human being in Christ outweighs the
bad news of sin, corruption and condemnation received from
Adam. In Christ, God has extended his mercy to all men in

every generation. God has paid for sin by offering His only begotten Son as a ransom for all (1 Timothy 2:6). The death of Christ was a sin offering. God gave the life of His Son as a free gift for the salvation of all who would believe:

> "And this is the record, that God hath given to us eternal life, and this life is in his Son. He that hath the Son hath life; and he that hath not the Son of God hath not life" (1 John 5:11-12).

> "For God has bound all men over to disobedience so that he may have mercy on them all. Oh, the depth of the riches of the wisdom and knowledge of God! How unsearchable his judgments, and his paths beyond tracing out!" (Romans 11:32-33).

Jesus is man's representative and every man's substitute. In Him every man was punished. The wrath of God against the sins of mankind was appeased and His indignation satisfied. Jesus died for every man and by that every man died in His death:

> "For the love of Christ constraineth us; because we thus judge, that if one died for all, then were all dead" (2 Corinthians 5:15).

Further, God gave His Son as a propitiation for all sins: "And He is the propitiation for our sins: and not for our sins only, but the sins of the whole world" (1 John 2:2). God made His Son who knew no sin, to be sin for all, so that all who may believe be made the righteousness of God in Him (2 Corinthians 5:21). John expressed the love of God in the following statement:

> "He that believeth on him is not condemned: but he that believeth not is condemned already, because he hath not believed in the name of the only begotten Son of God.

> And this is the condemnation, that light is come into the

world, and men loved darkness rather than light, because their deeds were evil" (John 3:16-19).

It is not the will of God that any man should perish, rather, that all may be saved which includes you and me. God takes no delight in the death of any man. Only one man, Jesus Christ, was born to die; every one else was born to live. This is why Paul in his letter to Timothy encouraged all Christians to pray for the salvation of all men:

"I exhort therefore, that, first of all, supplications, prayers, intercessions, and giving of thanks, be made for all men; for kings, and for all that are in authority; that we may lead a quiet and peaceable life in all godliness and honesty.

For this is good and acceptable in the sight of God our Saviour; who will have all men to be saved, and to come unto the knowledge of the truth. For there is one God, and one mediator between God and men, the man Christ Jesus" (1 Timothy 2:1-5).

The Cross of Calvary says it all. Calvary is what God said and did about all the sins committed by fallen man in the past, present and future. The cross of Jesus is the meeting place of the sins of mankind, the wrath of God, the grace and mercy of God, and the punishment for sins. The vicarious death of the Son of God on the cross provided emancipation and expiation of sins committed in the present, past, and future for all who choose to believe; His death provides new life with the promise of the Holy Spirit.

The outcome of what happened on the cross was peace and goodwill toward men. Sin, death, and Satan were totally defeated at the Cross of Calvary. In fact, neither Satan nor the rulers of this age understood the events of the cross, for if they had, they would not have crucified the Lord of glory (1 Corinthians 2:8).

The resurrection of Jesus Christ is also very important for Christians. If Jesus had not risen again from the dead, to confess

Him as Lord and Savior would have been in vain. Christians would have been liars in claiming that God raised Jesus Christ from the dead. Then, we Christians are fools because we believe and claim a man who died two thousand years ago to be our Lord and Savior. Christianity would have been like one of the many false religions:

> "And if Christ be not risen, then is our preaching vain, and your faith is also vain. Yea, and we are found false witnesses of God; because we have testified of God that he raised up Christ: whom he raised not up, if so be that the dead rise not. For if the dead rise not, then is not Christ raised.
>
> And if Christ be not raised, your faith is vain; ye are yet in your sins. Then they also which are fallen asleep in Christ are perished. If in this life only we have hope in Christ, we are of all men most miserable. But now is Christ risen from the dead, and become the firstfruits of them that slept" (1 Corinthians 15:14-20).

But, to God be the glory, Jesus did rise again from the dead. He was only in the grave for three days, for death could not hold Him captive. Having no sin of His own, death had no power over Him. Today He is alive, well, and highly exalted (Romans 1:4; 4:25). Only God can save, so if Jesus Christ is not what He claims to be or what the Bible portrays Him as being (equal with God and God), then He cannot save any man (cf. Titus 1:4; 2:13; 3:6; 2 Peter 1:1; 3:18).

Jesus' resurrection proved that He was indeed God's anointed; the Savior-Messiah, and the sinless Son of God. The resurrection also proved that the redemption work accomplished on the cross on behalf of man was accepted by God, and that God was well pleased and satisfied with Him and the work he has done. Further, His resurrection extolled Him above every creature — above angels and men.

The presence of the rotten bones and flesh (skeletons) in the tombstones of all religious leaders ever known in history is an indication they died as sinners and were no Saviors. They were not even qualified for what they claim to be. The only man who died and rose again from the dead and is alive forever is our Lord and Savior Jesus Christ. There is only one Savior for the human race and not many saviors.

There are many false Christs, but only one true Christ, who is Jesus Christ, the son of the living God. His earthly name Jesus, means Savior. His surname Christ means the anointed one or Messiah. The double title is an affirmation of His deity, which also differentiates Him from all other self-proclaimed saviors and prophets. Christians know Jesus Christ as the God-Man — a man who is fully God and fully man.

Every man in need of God's salvation is required to have faith in Jesus Christ. Faith is a gift from God and comes through the Gospel of Jesus Christ. Faith gained through the Gospel becomes personal faith, and with that, the believing sinner can accept the faith of Jesus Christ. He can accept all that Jesus accomplished for him through His redemptive and substitution death.

The Holy Spirit who is the dispenser of all faith is willing and ready to give to all who seek to know and come to God through Jesus Christ. Again, beware that the salvation God has provided for all mankind in Christ is not universalism; every man must first believe and accept the substitution and vicarious death of Jesus to be saved.

According to the word of God, "whoever believeth that Jesus is the Christ is born of God." And anyone who denies that Jesus is the Christ is considered to be a liar and antichrist (1 John 2:22):

"Whosoever believeth that Jesus is the Christ is born of God: and every one that loveth him that begat loveth him also that is begotten of him" (1 John 5:1).

To believe that Jesus is Christ is to receive Him as portrayed in Scripture: the anointed of God and Savior of the world. It is also to identify Him as the Christ; the expected Jewish

Messiah whose coming fulfills all prophesies. Anyone who says he believes must believe from the heart. Belief must exceed the sphere of sensible observation and beyond mere intellectual assent and acknowledgement. Lastly, such must be evidenced by acceptance and confession.

Until Jesus came, the Mosaic Law served as God's standard of righteousness for all men. But, when He fully fulfilled the law, the law was laid to rest forever. Jesus was made a curse for all humanity by dying on a shameful cross; therefore, all who come to God through His faith are redeemed from the curse of the Law (Galatians 3:19; Romans 10:4). They are dead to the law, and it does not matter whose law.

Righteousness in the sight of God is not found in natural religion and neither is it found in revealed religion (Romans 1:19,20; 3:1-2). It is only found in the Gospel of Christ or in Christ Jesus (Romans 1:16-17). The Gospel is God's love letter to the world. The Gospel reveals two important blessings for mankind: one, that Jesus died for our offenses; two, He was raised again for our Justification.

God declared His righteousness when He punished the sins of mankind in the person of His Holy Son. As a result, God is just in justifying any sinner who places his faith in His Son. This is the central message of the Gospel of Christ; if one died for all, then all died (2 Corinthians 5:14). As already mentioned, Jesus Christ is the glory of God personified (John 1:14).

Anyone who is willing can meet the holy requirements of God through Christ Jesus; Jesus Christ is the one stop for all human needs. In Him, there is an abundant grace and provision for all who come to God to be saved from their sins (Romans 3:24). According to the Scriptures "by the righteousness and obedience of one man (Jesus Christ) shall many be made righteous" (Romans 5:15-19). What qualifies a man as holy or righteous is not his own works but, by his faith in the faith of the only Son of God: "For therein is the righteousness of God is revealed from faith to faith" (Romans 1:17; cf. 4:25):

> "Even the righteousness of God which is by faith of Jesus Christ unto all and upon all them that believe: for there is no difference" (Romans 3:22).

As already stated, belief must be evidenced or followed by confession; you must establish your belief by confessing the same. Believing and confessing Jesus Christ as Lord and Savior is all that is required for any sinner to be saved (born again). When your faith joins the faith of Jesus Christ (Romans 1:17; 3:22), there is the imputation of sin to the righteous Lamb of God and conversely, imputation of righteousness to you.

Each and every believer seeking to be born again must demonstrate agreement and acknowledgement to the truth believed by professing the same. Faith is imputed as righteousness to all those who come to God through Christ (Acts 2:36). Confessing Jesus as Lord is the voice of a heart that is full of faith; remember, words are expression of thoughts. Belief is acceptance, and confession is a sign; hence, belief and confession ratifies the completed work of Christ on your behalf.

By your faith and confession, God is free to transfer all that Jesus has done and accomplished into your account; they become yours.

Do what the Gospel says

Now, follow the instructions from the word of God; just do what the scripture says:

> "But what saith it? The word is nigh thee, even in thy mouth, and in thy heart: that is, the word of faith, which we preach; that if thou shalt confess with thy mouth the Lord Jesus, and shalt believe in thine heart that God hath raised him from the dead, thou shalt be saved.
>
> For with the heart man believeth unto righteousness; and with the mouth confession is made unto salvation. For the scripture saith, whosoever believeth on him shall not be ashamed. For there is no difference between the Jew and the Greek:

for the same Lord over all is rich unto all that call upon him. For whosoever shall call upon the name of the Lord shall be saved" (Romans 10:8-13; cf. Revelations 3:20).

Jesus cannot be your Savior if you are ashamed to be identified with Him. Open your mouth and confess Him as your Lord and Savior right now — say it. Also, ask Him to forgive you all your sins. By this confession, you secure your name in the Lamb's book of life (Revelation 20:15; 19:9). If you are in doubt as to what to say let me help you.

Here is a sample prayer, feel free to use as your own:

Lord Jesus, thank you for dying for my salvation. Forgive me all my sins and cleanse me with thy precious blood. I from this moment accept you as my Lord and personal Savior. Thank you for saving me. Amen.

Congratulations if you did! Jesus said the new birth is like the passing wind, the wind can only be heard or observed, but cannot be seen or explained. So go ahead and enjoy your new life in Christ. You have obeyed the voice of God, and done exactly what He said you should do. Be assured that God has also done His part. You are set for life here and hereafter. Accept your salvation and never doubt again. God is faithful:

"Faithful is he that calleth you, who also will do it" (1 Thessalonians 5:24).

You are born again by believing and ratifying the same by your confession; consider yourself a Christian from this moment. Isn't it amazing? Is it that simple? Yes, this is the way God works. If you need further enlightenment on how to be saved, I recommend you read my book "A Second Chance." If you were not sure that you were a Christian when you first got baptized or have never been baptized in water (with water), then get baptized:

"All things are possible to him that believeth" (Mark 9:23).

Now, before I conclude this important chapter, let me make it easy for you to remember some of the blessings that are your possession as a Christian. This is who you are now by virtue of your new birth; this is what all Christians have in common:

1. Justified (declared righteous) by faith (Romans 3:24)

2. Possess the love of God (1 John 3:14; 5:1)

3. Have Vital union with Christ (2 Corinthians 13:5)

4. Sins forgiven; past, present and future (Ephesians 1:7; Colossians 1:14)

5. New creature (2 Corinthians 5:17)

6. Born again; second birth (John 3:13)

7. Washed, Cleansed (John 3:5; Titus 3:5; 1 Peter 2:9)

8. Sanctified (1 Corinthians 6:11; Titus 2:14; Romans 16;15; Hebrews 12:6-11; 1 Peter 1:7)

9. Possess the Spirit of adoption (Galatians 4:4,5)

10. Child of God (Romans 8:14)

11. The righteousness of God (2 Corinthians 5:21)

12. Alive unto God (reception of new life, Ephesians 2:1,5; 1 John 5:12)

13. Saved by grace

14. Possess a new name, saint (Ephesians 2:12,19; Romans 1:7; Ephesians 2:19; 1 Thessalonians 3:13).

15. Immediate access to God (Hebrews 10:19,20)

16. Peace with God (Romans 5:1)

17. Possess the peace of God (John 14:27; Ephesians 2:12-14,17)

18. Contentment (2 Timothy 1:12; Hebrews 13:5)

19. Indwelt by the Spirit (John 14:17; 1 John 2:20, 27; 3:24)

20. Blessed (Ephesians 1:3; Galatians 3:14)

21. Reception of a new nature (2 Peter 1:4)

22. Possess the mind of God (Philippians 2:5)

23. Victory over sin, devil and the world (Romans 8:37; 1 John 3:9; 5:4,18)

24. New destiny (John 14:1; Philippians 1:23; 1 Thessalonians 4:16,17; Revelations 21:27)

25. Passed from death to life (1 John 3:14)

26. Possess eternal redemption (Hebrews 9:12)

27. Jesus your advocate in heaven (Romans 8:34; Hebrews 7:25; 9:24; 1 John 2:1)

28. Citizens of heaven

29. Full assurance of hope (Hebrews 6:11)

    Holiness of life (1 John 5:18)

30. Holy Spirit your advocate on earth (Luke 12:12; Romans 8:34)

31. Reward for righteous living (2 Corinthians 4:17)

32. God's property (1 Corinthians 6:19-20; 1 Peter 1:18-19)

33. Ambassadors for Christ (2 Corinthians 5:20)

34. Constant protection from all foes (Romans 8:31)

In conclusion, "Praise be to the God and Father of our Lord Jesus Christ! In His great mercy He has given us new birth into a living hope through the resurrection of Jesus Christ from the dead" (1 Peter 1:3). Every Christian is blood bought, blood washed, and Spirit born. Every Christian is born again; if you are not born again, then you are not a Christian and it does not matter how good or religious you may be.

Every Christian is born of God, born by the Holy Spirit, and born by the will of God. To be born of the transcended

God is to be born transcended. The good news is that every human being has the opportunity to be born again, and all it takes is to accept God's free gift of His Son Jesus Christ.

Through regeneration (spiritual birth) every Christian is a new man, new creature, and complete. Never would our new man need any improvement or repair (Colossians 3:10). Regeneration is an inside work. Although the body, environment, neighbors, workmates, friends and family remain the same, inside is a brand new man. If this is what it takes to be a Christian, can anybody deny that the Christian life is transcended? Now, let us talk about other important aspects of This Transcended Life.

Chapter Three

 God is indeed wonderful. It appears every step a believer takes towards God is met with a wonder, a miracle, or a mystery; God is indeed awesome. If any man finds it hard to accept or believe the new birth of a child of God, then here is another. Everyone that is born of God is indwelt by the transcended God. Each individual Christian is indwelt by God the Holy Spirit. Spirit born, Christians are Spirit indwelt. With the birth of a Christian, God has indeed tabernacled with man.

The body of a Christian is the temple of the Holy God and the same is true of every individual Christian. The blessed fact that our body is the temple of God has two sides. One, that he is ours; the other, that we are His. The gift of Christ to all who are born again is the indwelling Spirit:

> "What? Know ye not that your body is the temple of the Holy Ghost which is in you, which ye have of God, and ye are not your own? (1 Corinthians 6:19).

The glorious nature of rebirth is that the Holy Spirit does not just regenerate and leave, but He remains with the believer for life. By virtue of the new birth, God has chosen the human body to be His dwelling place — to be His home. It was absolutely impossible for the Holy God to dwell in the former sin-ridden, depraved heart, but now everything has changed. God is not just with us, but for us and in us forever. To be honest, the highest attainment in the life of every human being is to be born and indwelt by God.

Christians carry God with them everywhere they go; He is closer to them than the hair on the skin. Amazing, isn't it? God dwelling with man is the true Abraham blessing that was promised to every believer who is justified by faith:

> **"He redeemed us in order that the blessing given to Abraham might come to the Gentiles through Christ Jesus, so that by faith we might receive the promise of the Spirit" (Galatians 3:14).**

Alongside our newly created spirit has come the Spirit of the Lord God. Dwelling with man has been the plan of God from eternity past (Genesis 3:8). The desire of God is to be with His people forever: "And let them make me a sanctuary that I may dwell among them (Exodus 25:8). The same Spirit, who is the source of our confession, has made our human bodies His dwelling place (1 John 4:2):

> **"Hereby know we that we dwell in him, and he in us, because he hath given us of his Spirit" (1 John 4:13).**

Our union with the Son of God is that He lives in us and us in Him. We are in Jesus, Jesus is in the Father and we are in the Father by Christ Jesus. Jesus said the Spirit would teach us of this union with the triune God:

> **"At that day ye shall know that I am in my Father, and ye in me, and I in you" (John 14:20).**

To put it bluntly, if a man does not have the Spirit of God, he does not have Christ, and neither does he belong to God. Indwelling Spirit is the only proof of belonging to God:

> **"Now if any man have not the Spirit of Christ, he is none of his" (Romans 8:9).**

Regeneration is very private, for no man is privileged to witness his own spiritual birth or the birth of another and neither is any human eye honored to see the Holy One dwelling in the heart of His saint. By His own indwelling presence, God has gloriously magnified the human body in spite of its mortality and fragility. Everything God does, He does it so well; wisdom crowns all His works, Amen.

With God at home in the body, Christians are admonished to be careful as to how they use and treat their bodies. No Christian can afford to make the body which is now the temple of God unclean, and neither can they mutilate or treat the body any way. The believer's body must be kept holy because the Holy God lives in it:

"If any man defile the temple of God, him shall God destroy; for the temple of God is holy, which temple ye are" (1 Corinthians 3:16-17).

Believe it or not, no man can enter into heaven by mistake or by pretense. Of course, anyone can profess to be a Christian, but that is before men and not God. Indwelling God shines brilliantly within every Christian. The reason the world, and even ourselves, do not see the beaming light of His presence is because; the excellence of His power is clothed in mortal dust. However, a day is coming, and very soon, when all creation shall see us; for we shall shine brighter than the sun at noon day, and every Christian shall be glorified. We shall be clothed with immortality.

Sometimes we ignorantly point to brick and mortar as the house of God and forget that man is rather the house or the temple of God. When Christians gather to worship God comes with them because He lives in everyone of them. But, also remember, when they leave, they leave with Him: "For where two or three are gathered together in my name, there am I in the midst of them" (Mathew 18:20).

Technically, Christians do not need a specially designed building or church building in order to pray or worship God. Christians can worship God at any place they may choose at any time. This could be the open field, a private home, on a boat, etc., or any place of convenience. Wherever a Christian is, there is God. When Christians gather together in the private home for prayer or fellowship, they are guaranteed the presence of the Lord Jesus.

The God who made the universe does not live in temples built with human hands; the human body is His preferred home:

"God that made the world and all things therein, seeing that he is Lord of heaven and earth, dwelleth not in temples made with hands" (Acts 17:24).

Jesus is physically in heaven; however, He dwells spiritually in the heart of all His chosen, blood bought and blood washed saints by the indwelling Holy Spirit. Remember, the Holy Spirit is also the spirit of Jesus Christ and the spirit of God (Romans 8:9-10). This truth is awesome. In fact, it brings to my mind the tabernacle or the structure that Moses was instructed by God to erect so that He may dwell among them. This structure was in three parts: the outer court, the holy place, and the holy of holies.

The people of Israel were allowed into the outer court, but not into the holy place. The priests were allowed into the holy place, but not into the holy of holies. Only the high priest was allowed to enter the Holiest place once a year and on the Day of Atonement and even then, he could not enter until after much preparation, cleansing and sacrifices without which he would not return alive.

The holiness of God was such that even the slightest breach in the handling of the structure, furniture and the sacrifices was punishable by instant death. Other times, the presence of the Lord in the tabernacle became so strong that even the priest could not enter. But, Hallelujah, Amen! This same holy, fearful and terrible God, before whom the people of Israel trembled exceedingly, has made His home with man; the body of His saints is now His holy dwelling place.

Looking backward historically to the dwelling places of God, we see after Moses' tabernacle came King Solomon's Temple and finally the Son of God. Jesus Christ is the true tabernacle of God. He is the man after whom all the previous temples and tabernacle were modeled. Jesus Christ is the eternal Word, which became flesh: "The word became flesh, and tabernacled among us" (John 1:14 Revised Version). Jesus Christ has made it possible for man not only to become the sons of God, but also the church and the temple of the living God.

Oh what a glory, what an amazing grace! It is a great honor to be chosen of God — to be chosen to be His sacred dwelling place. What a privilege and a friend we have in Jesus. If only Christians can understand who they truly are? I believe we can impart the world in a much greater way. In short, living believers are now the new temples of the Living God:

> **"And I heard a great voice out of heaven saying, Behold, the tabernacle of God is with men, and he will dwell with them, and they shall be his people, and God himself shall be with them, and be their God"** (Revelation 21:3).

I pray that every Christian would awaken to the truth of the reality of His indwelling presence. Sometimes Christians stumble over Psalm 51:11 "Cast me not away from thy presence; and take not thy Holy Spirit from me." Under the Old Testament, the Spirit work was outward and intermittent, for example, He came upon certain men for special purposes, and left when the purpose was accomplished, but this is not the case with the Christian. Under the New Testament, the Spirit work is inward, and His presence abiding:

> **"And I will pray the Father, and He shall give you another Comforter, and he may abide with you forever. Even the Spirit of truth; whom the world cannot receive, because it seeth him not, neither knoweth him: But ye know him; for he dwelleth with you, and shall be in you"** (John 14:16-17).

Christians must see themselves exceptionally favored, and rightly live up to divine expectation. We must consider ourselves greatly blessed:

"Blessed be the God and Father of our Lord Jesus Christ, who hath blessed us with all spiritual blessings in heavenly places in Christ" (Ephesians 1:3).

We are God's handiwork, His masterpiece and dwelling place. Jesus said, "we are the salt and the light of this world." We must believe all that God says about us in His holy word; we must renew our mind with the truth of God's holy Word through the precious Holy Spirit. It is extremely important for each of us to know who we are in Christ Jesus:

"But you are a chosen people, a royal priesthood, a holy nation, a people belonging to God, that you may declare the praises of him who called you out of darkness into his wonderful light" (1 Peter 2:9).

Every Christian has been chosen for a special purpose; each individual Christian has his own special place in God. None were randomly picked. We were not collectively chosen like a bunch of fruit. Every one of us was deliberately hand picked by God and like precious stones are being built together upon the foundation of the apostles and the prophets — Christ Jesus being the chief cornerstone as a permanent dwelling place of God by the Holy Spirit (Ephesians 2:21,23).

Beloved, at this juncture, I sense I must stop and pray, let us pray this prayer which the apostle Paul also prayed for the church together. I pray that God:

"Would grant you, according to the riches of his glory, to be strengthened with might by his Spirit in the inner man; that Christ may dwell in your hearts by faith; that ye, being rooted and grounded in love.

May be able to comprehend with all saints what is the breadth, and length, and depth, and height; and to know

the love of Christ, which passeth knowledge, that ye
might be filled with all the fulness of God.

Now unto him that is able to do exceeding abundantly
above all that we ask or think, according to the power
that worketh in us, unto him be glory in the church by
Christ Jesus throughout all ages, world without end.
Amen" (Ephesians 3:16-21).

Continue to pray that the Spirit of truth (Holy Spirit)
would make you conscious of His indwelling presence 24 hours
a day and 7 days a week. I know the truth as revealed may be
hard on the mind and even for some to accept, but God said,
only the truth can set us free. Spiritual truths are always beyond
natural reasoning; they can only be accepted by spiritual people,
by those who are indwelt by the Holy Spirit.

Only the mind and heart that is after God can be receptive
to the truth as given by the Spirit. For the mature Christians,
and for the spirit that is inundated by the Spirit, all that God
had revealed is open and accepted:

"Now we have received, not the spirit of the world, but
the spirit which is of God; that we might know the things
that are freely given to us of God. Which things also we
speak, not in the words which man's wisdom teacheth,
but which the Holy Ghost teacheth; comparing spiritual
things with spiritual.

But the natural man receiveth not the things of the Spirit
of God: for they are foolishness unto him: neither can he
know them, because they are spiritually discerned.

But he that is spiritual judgeth all things, yet he himself
is judged of no man. For who hath known the mind of the
Lord, that he may instruct him? but we have the mind of
Christ" (1 Corinthians 2:12-16).

How a Christian knows he is a Christian is by the inner
witness of the Holy Spirit. The Spirit Himself, unceasingly

witnesses to our newly created human spirit that we are the sons of God. From within, He assures each of us of our sonship and new position in God's family. From within, Spirit talks to spirit. A hymnist once sang this song: "if you ask me how I know He lives? He lives within my Heart," and this is true for every Christian. Jesus furnishes evidence of His presence in each of us by the presence of the dwelling Spirit in the heart:

> **"The Spirit itself beareth witness with our spirit, that we are the children of God" (Romans 8:16).**

> **"And because ye are sons, God hath sent forth the Spirit of his Son into your hearts, crying, Abba, Father" (Galatians 4:6).**

> **"And he that keepeth his commandments dwelleth in him, and he in him. And hereby we know that he abideth in us, by the Spirit which he hath given us" (1 John3:24).**

Bought by the blood of Jesus Christ, every Christian is God's personal property. The presence of the Spirit in the heart is His own seal of ownership. The Spirit comes in at the moment of salvation to certify a completed transaction (1 Peter 1:18-19; 1 Corinthians 6:20); the Spirit is the seal of genuineness and authentication and also the believer's security and surety. There can be no mistake in the eyes of God concerning those who are His:

> **"Who hath also sealed us, and given the earnest of the Spirit in our hearts" (2 Corinthians 1:22).**

Further, the Spirit is an 'earnest' deposit in the heart of the believer. The Spirit is God's down payment and the pledge of our redemption. As a deposit, His indwelling presence guarantees that God would definitely preserve and take care of that which is His until the redemption of the purchased possession (Ephesians 1:14). God guarantees by His indwelling presence that each of us shall be glorified on the day of Christ (Romans 8:29). God is faithful; He would surely bring to completion all that which He has begun in each of us.

Furthermore, Christians are said to have the Holy Spirit as first-fruits. This means, the Spirit is the first installment and a promise that more is to be expected. More blessings are stored up for the believer, but here is the good news, these blessings are immediately available to every believer by virtue of His indwelling Presence:

"Now we have received, not the spirit of the world, but the spirit which is of God; that we might know the things that are freely given to us of God" (1 Corinthians 2:12):

"And not only they, but ourselves also, which have the firstfruits of the Spirit, even we ourselves groan within ourselves, waiting for the adoption, to wit, the redemption of our body" (Romans 8:23).

Technically, a farmer's first-fruits are the initial harvesting of his first-ripened crops. This initial harvest can be said to be his installment, which is an indication of the type of harvest that is soon to follow. Likewise, the indwelling Holy Spirit is the believer's first installment; a foretaste of the glory here and hereafter (Romans 8:17).

Again, the presence of the indwelling Spirit is the believer's anointing and power. Jesus was anointed of the Holy Spirit and so is every one that He calls into His fellowship (Acts 10:38). The same anointing that was on Him is on all His disciples. Set apart by God and for God, every Christian is anointed. The oil with which both Jesus and Christians are anointed is the Holy Spirit (2 Corinthians 1:21). Every Christian is indwelt by the Anointed One:

"But the anointing which ye have received of him abideth in you, and ye need not that any man teach you: but as the same anointing teacheth you of all things, and is

truth, and is no lie, and even as it hath taught you, ye
shall abide in him" (1 John 2:27)

―――――――――

**"But ye have an unction from the Holy One, and ye know
all things' (1 John 2:20)**

The word 'unction' in the above passage, literally means a
specially prepared anointing oil (Exodus 30:25; 40:9; Leviticus
21:10). The anointing which New Testament Christians have
received or experienced by the indwelling Spirit is the same as
that which was experienced by the Old Testament saints. The
same Holy Spirit is at work in both cases.

For example, Old Testament kings and priest were anointed
with specially-prepared anointing oil. By pouring the anointing
oil on the head of a king or priest, they were said to be set apart
by God for special use. In most cases, this act was accompanied
immediately by the presence or the movement of the Spirit by
which some experienced power and renewal. Recipients became
new and empowered for the task for which they were chosen.

This experience is the same for every New Testament saint.
Chosen by God, Christians have unction from the Holy One to:

**"Show forth the praises of him who hath called you out
of darkness into his marvelous light" (1 Peter 2:9).**

Brethren, we should be very grateful to God for giving us
His Holy Spirit. The Spirit indwelling is like God has given
us part of Himself to come to Him (a little heaven to come to
heaven). The Spirit does not give a little of Himself; then, little
by little until we get all of Him; no, this is not the case. At the
moment of salvation, He comes in fully or wholly to dwell with
our new spirit. Only God can testify of God as a result, God-
the Father has sent God-the Holy Spirit to testify of God-the
Son in the heart of His saints and to a dying world.

I pray you do not confuse this early stage of the Spirit
incoming and indwelling with that which is experienced by those

seeking the gifts of the Spirit and that which was experienced by the apostles on the day of Pentecost. I shall talk about that later in this book. What I have so far talked about is that which all believers automatically receive at regeneration. Each individual Christian is fully indwelt by God at the moment of Salvation (cf. John 20:22). You do not have to ask for the Spirit to come in, and neither does He need your permission. You gave Him the permission when you accepted Jesus Christ as your Lord and personal Savior; when you opened the door of your heart to God.

Your acceptance was your signature permitting Jesus to be everything to you: To be your savior, helper, leader, instructor, friend, power of attorney, master, Lord and God now and forever more: "Behold, I stand at the door, and knock: if any man hear my voice, and open the door, I will come in to him, and will sup with him, and he with me" (Revelation 3:20). And this supper (partying) together goes on until it's fulfillment at the marriage supper of the Lamb (Revelation 19:9).

In conclusion, without the indwelling presence of the Spirit of Christ, no man can claim to be born again or even say he belongs to God. Born of the Spirit, we are fully indwelt by God: "Whosoever shall confess that Jesus is the Son of God, God dwelleth in him, and he in God" (1 John 4:15). By His Spirit, each of us would know that Jesus indeed lives in the hearts of His saints, and for that matter trinity lives in every Christian:

> **"Hereby we know that we dwell in Him, and He in us, because He has given us His Spirit" (1 John 4:13; cf. Revelation 3:20).**

Jesus Christ, by His spirit, comes to live in us and we live in Him by faith. This union with the triune God is solid and forever, and nothing in this world or in the world to come or by any means separate, disrupt or break this bond of love. The power of Christians is that the triune God is in and with them forever. The Spirit indwelling is not only limited to subjective experience; He is there, in us whether or not we feel Him.

Now, I want you to pause and reflect on what you have discovered from these two chapters. Get outside and take a look at your surroundings; take a look at the sky, the trees and landscape. Reflect over the fact that the God who made all these is your Father and also over the fact that He lives inside you. Finally, ask yourself, if God lives in me, then who am I? In Christ dwelleth all the fullness of the Godhead bodily; and you are complete and full in Him.

Chapter Four

LED BY THE SPIRIT

 This chapter must be studied very carefully if you truly desire to have victory over sin; if you want to experience a deeper walk with God. Spiritual growth suffers where doctrinal warnings are ignored or not taken seriously. The secret of living a holy and sanctified Christian life is to be led by the Holy Spirit. Born by the Spirit and indwelt by the Spirit, the wisest thing each of us can do is to submit ourselves to the control, power and leadership of the indwelling Spirit.

It can never be that we should be the boss of our life while the Lord is at home with us:

> "For as many as are led by the Spirit of God, they are the sons of God" (Romans 8:14).

There is one characteristic quality of all who are led by the Holy Spirit and that quality is that they walk in all the ways of righteousness; they maintain a consistent life of holiness. They walk and talk like heavenly beings. Their language is inundated with spiritual insight.

Having the Spirit means having the mind of Christ; it means having thoughts, behavioral patterns, and lifestyles that are

consistent to that of Jesus Christ. It also means having desires
and affections that are God-centered and heavenly-minded. It
means being inundated by the Spirit — completely possessed,
pervaded and permeated by the Spirit of Christ:

> **"May be able to comprehend with all the saints what is
> the breadth, and length, and depth, and height; And to
> know the love of Christ, which passeth knowledge, that
> ye might be filled with all the fullness of God"** (Ephe-
> sians 3:18-19).

The question of being led by the Spirit is extremely important,
for without that, defeat is certain. Sin in the flesh can only be
defeated when a Christian is led by the Spirit (Romans 7:20). Every
Christian must be aware of the presence of sin dwelling in the flesh
and the dangerous role it seeks to play in the transcended life. As
already touched on, God did not do away with the old sinful nature
during regeneration. Instead, He created a completely new man —
a qualitatively new creature. God did not repair, renovate or reform
the old nature, He left it alone.

This means that every Christian has the old man living
alongside the new man in the same old mortal frame (body).
This also means every Christian possesses two natures: the old
sinful nature and the new divine nature. Remember, the old
man is what we were spiritually before we became born again.
I guess the bible's own definition of the old man is better; I do
not think anyone can improve on that:

> **"That ye put off concerning the former conversation, the
> old man, which is corrupt according to deceitful lusts"**
> (Ephesians 4:22).

The two natures living together is a problem for every
Christian from the moment of salvation. The old man is of the
flesh and seeks the things of the flesh, but our new man is holy
and desires the things of God. The old man has an advantage
because nothing has really changed for him. He is in his old
familiar suit (mortal body), the same environment and the

same evil friend, the devil. Friends and neighbors do not change simply because we become Christians. This means our new man has a potent contender from day one.

To tell you the truth, the new man, despite being created in righteousness and true holiness is no match for the old man. But, God who is infinitely wise has this problem solved by the presence of the Holy Spirit. We do not have to worry or fear; we would not have to fight sin in the flesh. Our indwelling Spirit takes over the fight. Any concerns, struggle or conflict with the old man, is addressed by the indwelling Spirit.

The Christian's battle with sin in the flesh is the battle of the Lord. To be candid, as long as each individual Christian follows the leading of the Spirit or allows the Spirit to be in control, the old man is finished. Sin expresses itself through the mind and the members of our body i.e., the tongue, hands and feet. Indwelling sin, alive and well in the flesh, would continue to try to use our body to his advantage. He will try to interfere with our new life, and for this reason, each of us must be led by the Spirit. We must resist the devil at all cost:

"Resist the devil, and he will fly from you (James 4:7):

No believer on his own can defeat sin because to fight the devil by our own power is a joke: "Wherefore let him that thinketh he standeth take heed lest he falls" (1 Corinthians 10:12). The conflict between our old nature and the new nature is a conflict between the Spirit and the flesh. The Spirit and victory go hand in hand and so is the flesh and defeat. If we choose the way of the Spirit it is victory, but if we choose the flesh it is defeat:

"Know ye not, that to whom ye yield yourselves servants to obey, his servants ye are to whom ye obey; whether of sin unto death, or of obedience unto righteousness?" (Romans 6:16).

Through the Spirit, each of us must resist sin's effort to impose its lifestyle. Sin must not be allowed to use our body as a

vehicle of expression to the displeasure of our Lord and Savior.
None of us can afford to grieve the Spirit by whom we are sealed
unto salvation. God forbid that any Christian should yield his will
and the members of his body to the works of unrighteousness.
Yielding our will to the mastery of sin is death, but, yielding to
the obedience of Christ is righteousness and peace:

> **"But now being made free from sin, and becoming ser-
> vants of God, ye have your fruit unto holiness, and in the
> end everlasting life" (Romans 6:22).**

Born again, we must refuse sin: "God sending Jesus Christ
in the likeness of sinful flesh and for sin, condemned sin in the
flesh" (Romans 8:3). Jesus condemned sin by His death on
the Cross, and this He did so that Christians can live holy in
conduct and service through the indwelling Spirit. As far as
God is concerned, the principles of sin and death are dead in
the believer; the old, corrupt, and decaying man or unregenerate
self is forever rejected. With the arrival of the new man, the old
man is discarded, and considered dead or abandoned.

Every Christian must know that Christians are dead to
sin because of our identification or union with Christ. Dead
to sin means dead to the guilt of sin. It means sin has no longer
control or power over us. No Christian can continue in sin,
because we are born, indwelt and led by the Spirit of God. Life
in sin cannot co-exist with death to sin (Romans 6:3). Buried
with Christ through baptism, sin cannot make any legal claim
on any Christian:

> **"God forbid. How shall we, that are dead to sin, live any
> longer therein?" (Romans 6:2).**

Further, through baptism, Christians were buried with
Jesus Christ unto His death and were resurrected together to
a new life. As a result, Christians are forever separated from
sin. Resurrected life is transcended and is emptied of sin; it is
holiness and purity in life and service. It is the God kind of life;
a life that is eternal in quality and everlasting in duration:

"Whosoever is born of God doth not commit sin; for his seed remaineth in him: and he cannot sin, because he is born of God" (1 John 3:9).

On the cross, our old man was crucified with Jesus Christ, so that we may resurrect to a new man; a new beginning, a clean slate, and a fresh start:

" Knowing this, that our old man is crucified with him, that the body of sin might be destroyed, that henceforth we should not serve sin" (Romans 6:6).

Christians are under obligation not to live after the flesh, but after the Spirit. We are not debtors to the flesh, or to the lifestyle we had prior to salvation. Having the Spirit, no Christian can afford to walk after the flesh: "For to be carnally minded is death" (Romans 6:6):

"Therefore, brothers, we have an obligation—but it is not to the sinful nature, to live according to it" (Romans 8:12).

In the fall (Genesis 3), man rebelled against the rule of God; he sought to be his own boss. Instead, he became a slave to sin and Satan. Through rebirth, man is given another opportunity; a second chance to exercise trust, obedience and dependence on God.

To God be the glory for His kindness and mercy: "O the depth of the riches both of the wisdom and knowledge of God! How unsearchable are his judgments, and his ways past finding out!" (Romans 11:33). God has made foolish the wisdom of this world? Because:"After that in the wisdom of God the world by wisdom knew not God, it pleased God by the foolishness of preaching to save them that believe" (1 Corinthians 1:20-21). Truly, the ways of God are past finding; His ways are not our ways, neither His thoughts our thoughts (Isaiah 55:8).

The flesh being weak, is not subject to the Law of God:"the carnal mind is enmity against God: for it is not subject to the law of God, neither indeed can be (Romans 7:23); it stands to oppose any move towards holiness.

At times it breaks my heart when I hear Christians moaning under phrases like: 'But I am trying;' I am working hard on it;' 'I am only human;' etc. As a Christian you are not just human, you are the son of God; you are a spirit being — indwelt and empowered by the transcended God. You are no ordinary human being.

We must have under our belt the truth of what has happened or become of us. The Spirit is the believer's access to Jesus and Jesus is his access to the Father: "For through him we both have access by one Spirit unto the Father" (Ephesians 2:18). The ministry of the indwelling Spirit is to produce the life of Christ in and through every believer (Romans 8:29), and the duty of every Christian is to be led each day by the Holy Spirit. If the Spirit lives in us and we live in Him, then we are in union and communion with the Holy One:

> **"If we live in the Spirit, let us also walk in the Spirit" (1 John 3:24).**

To be led by the Spirit is great. This means we would know all the things that are freely given to us of God; we would know all the things that God has prepared for those who love Him; we would know the deep things of God; we would walk and speak of things as taught by God and not as the wisdom of men will dictate:

> **"However, as it is written: "No eye has seen, no ear has heard, no mind has conceived what God has prepared for those who love him" but God has revealed it to us by his Spirit.**

> **The Spirit searches all things, even the deep things of God. For who among men knows the thoughts of a man except the man's spirit within him? In the same way no one knows the thoughts of God except the Spirit of God.**

> **We have not received the spirit of the world but the Spirit who is from God, that we may understand what God has freely given us.**

This is what we speak, not in words taught us by human wisdom but in words taught by the Spirit, expressing spiritual truths in spiritual words" (1 Corinthians 2:9-13).

Further, we would never live in ignorance or in darkness, because the Spirit teaches us all things, and brings all things to remembrance. Furthermore, we shall be faithful witnesses, for not only does the Spirit reveal Christ in and to us but, He will also testify of Him through us (John 14:26). Further still, we would never be led astray by the sly of men when we are led by the Spirit of truth:

"But when he, the Spirit of truth, comes, he will guide you into all truth. He will not speak on his own; he will speak only what he hears, and he will tell you what is yet to come. He will bring glory to me by taking from what is mine and making it known to you.

All that belongs to the Father is mine. That is why I said the Spirit will take from what is mine and make it known to you" (John 16:13-15).

Transcended life is not possible without the Spirit, for it is the Spirit who makes the life of a Christian unique. Since God is transcended and therefore possesses transcended life, only He can make it known and empower the Christian to live the same. The daily life of a Christian is, or should be a miracle where the Spirit lives and rules.

Through Christ, Christians are released from the law which previously kept them bound and the purpose of this release is to give each individual Christian a new start. That henceforth we may serve God in the newness of the spirit. That we may serve God in a new way by the Holy Spirit of God (cf. John 4:23-4):

"Might present it to himself a glorious church, not having spot, or wrinkle, or any such thing; but that it should be holy and without blemish" (Ephesians 5:27).

A woman who has a husband is bound to her husband so long as he lives, but, if her husband dies she is free to marry another man and would not be considered an adulteress. Likewise, Christians are dead to the law; therefore they are free from the written codes of the law. They are free to be married to another, to Him who died for them. We are united with Him as his bride (Ephesians 5:25). Jesus is the life of every Christian.

As a result of our resurrection with Christ or by virtue of the new birth, Christians must reckon themselves dead to sin and alive to God. Each individual Christian must keep counting daily that he is dead to sin. We do not die daily; we died once with Christ and alive with Him to die no more, but we must count ourselves dead to sin and to the pleasures of this world daily; the truth of our deadness and freedom from the control and power of sin must be a daily reminder and acknowledgement.

We do not live to become holy, we are already as holy as can ever be, and no man can improve on that, but, we live daily to reckon it to be so. Sanctification is not to be holier and holier every day; rather, it is increasingly becoming aware that we are holy. It is the renewal of the mind; the mind of Christ must be the default. Each of us can absolutely depend on the indwelling Spirit to make this truth a practical daily realization. The work of the Spirit, if we allow Him, is to provide power to live the new life.

Our stand before God would never change; i.e., from holy to unholy, neither would our new man ever be corrupt, but to live out who we are in Christ is another. It is for this practical aspect of our salvation that the Spirit has come alongside as our helper and Lord. Sin dwelling in the flesh and aided by Satan, would continue to wage war within. However, we are guaranteed victory if only we are led by the Spirit.

Beloved, see how many quotations I have provided for you. Know and believe that these things I am sharing with you are revelations from the Lord and not of my own: "we speak the wisdom of God in a mystery, even the hidden wisdom, which God ordained before the world unto our glory" (1 Corinthians 2:7).

Anyone who is not born again is a master of his or her own life. Man without the Spirit of God is of the flesh; he lives by his own instincts and does the things that are pleasing to him. An arrogant and ignorant man is no different from the mentally ill.

We are born again to serve a new master, which is Christ. However, in order for this to happen, new things must be kept from old things:

> **"No man also seweth a piece of new cloth on an old garment: else the new piece that filled it up taketh away from the old, and the rent is made worse. And no man putteth new wine into old bottles: else the new wine doth burst the bottles, and the wine is spilled, and the bottles will be marred: but new wine must be put into new bottles"** (Mark 2:21-22).

Every Christian is called upon to put off deliberately and permanently the old man. We must throw away the old, filthy garments of uncontrolled temper, a settled feeling of habitual hate, revengeful resentment, boiling agitation, fiery outburst of temper, violent fits of rage, rejoicing in evil to others, vicious disposition, willful desire to injure others, slanderous talk, evil speaking, railing insults, reckless and bitter abuse, filthy speech, obscene speech, shameful speaking, foul-mouthed abuse, dirty epithets, and unclean stories. We must stop lying to God and to each other, period. There is no such thing as white lies; a lie is a lie, whether small, little or big. Every lie is dirty and must be thrown away for good. God does not regard sin with indifference:

> **"Lie not one to another, seeing that ye have put off the old man with his deeds"** (Colossians 3:9; cf. verses 1-8).

Further, other old stuff such as illicit sexual intercourse between unmarried partners, perverse sin, impurity in thought and speech, dirty desires, depraved passion, uncontrolled lust, evil desires, wicked cravings and sensualness beyond natural expression, greedy desire to have more, entire disregard for the right of others, worship of false gods and putting things in place of God must be thrown away through the Spirit.

Remember, even though Christians have been reckoned righteous on the merit of Christ, it is one thing to be declared righteous and another to live a practical holy life. Also, the impartation of a new spirit, new heart and cleansing at rebirth does not automatically translate into a practical holiness for the believer. Without the leading of the Spirit of God and the availability of His power, victory over the sins of the flesh is just not possible (Ezekiel 36:26-27).

Realistically, without the presence, influence and power of the indwelling Holy Spirit, there won't be any significant difference between the character of a Christian before and after rebirth; between the saint and the sinner; or the Christian and non-Christian. Jesus knew beforehand, that this problem will face his newly made people, and as a result prayed for the Spirit to come to us. Jesus sent a helper like Himself to be for, with and in us (John 17:20, 23). Christians are not in the flesh, but in the Spirit (Romans 8:9):

"This I say then, Walk in the Spirit, and ye shall not fulfil the lust of the flesh" (Galatians 5:16).

Every Christian must be led by the Spirit of God to experience daily victory over the flesh (Romans 6:11; 7:4; 8:13). We must pray for His will to replace our will: "Thy will be done," should be the daily prayer of every Christian. Remember, Transcended Life is life fully lived in the Spirit.

I must confess; to our shame, it appears despite all the hard work we exert trying to change or kick out old habits, we often fail miserably. In many occasions, we become despondent and slowly give up or even quit trying altogether. Others take the fight further by serious deprivations, mutilations and other painful treatment of their own bodies.

Truthfully, these acts are wonderful attempts by themselves but, they produce very little results, and in most cases, zero results. Some even take it further by blaming God for not helping enough. Instead of all these self-efforts, what we should be doing is calling upon the Spirit, in other words, allowing the Holy Spirit to deal with all unwanted habits. Simply, asking the Holy Spirit to uproot sins of the flesh as they surface or get exposed in our daily walk with God.

Only God can uproot sin and cause it not to grow again. Only God can uproot the weeds of sin and then plant the good fruit of holy habits. In the place of sin, He grows holy characters; the fruit of the Spirit are part of His attributes. We must employ the full services of our Lord and helper, for this purpose He came. He is best at destroying old habits; Old habits are not trimmed, the Spirit literally uproots them. Root, stem, branch and fruits are all taken away; sin is a principle, endemic and a potent enemy and must be completely destroyed.

Permit me to give you a practical example of how you should pray in your fight against sin. For example, instead of asking Him to help you get rid of sinful habits, ask Him to take the sinful habits away:

"For if ye live after the flesh, ye shall die: but if ye through the Spirit do mortify the deeds of the body, ye shall live" (Romans 8:13).

The Spirit did not come to help us do the fighting; He came to do the fighting. Your fight is His fight and your victory His victory; therefore, two of you cannot be fighting the same enemy at the same time. Remember, He is the Lord, He does not appreciate your help; He considers your help an intrusion, a setback and an interference. He is your boss, manager, power of attorney and representative in all things on earth, in the same way Jesus is your Lord and representative in heaven.

Our job is to rest in God's promises and let the Spirit do His work, do what He has come to do and is best at: "For all the promises of God in him are yea, and in him Amen, unto the glory of God by us" (2 Corinthians 1:20; cf. 7:1). Let us therefore call upon Him at all times and not only when there are crises, but even in times of peace and tranquility:

"In all thy ways acknowledge him, and he shall direct thy paths" (Proverbs 3:6).

Again, the Spirit represents us in all spiritual warfare; whether it is a fight against disease, sin, Satan, demons, poverty — you name it. He personalizes our fight if we let Him; further, the Spirit helps us in our prayers; He formats all our prayers in a way that is acceptable and favorable to God and guarantees results. All we need to do is to call upon God in faith:

"Likewise the Spirit also helpeth our infirmities: for we know not what we should pray for as we ought: but the Spirit itself maketh intercession for us with groanings which cannot be uttered" (Romans 8:26).

If any human being follows the path of the natural birth without a second birth, he would surely end up in the lake that burns with fire and brimstone (Revelation 21:8; mark 9:42-48). Likewise, if a Christian allows the flesh to interfere with the new life, he shall be reduced to a life of defeat and even premature death:

"For the flesh lusteth against the Spirit, and the Spirit against the flesh: and these are contrary the one to the other: so that ye cannot do the things that ye would" (Galatians 5:17).

Misunderstanding of this truth as explained in the Bible is the reason many Christians, even though dead to sin, are still engaged in sinful and shameful habits. It also explains why certain Christians live like the devil, yet are devoted to the service of God, and why some preachers preach one thing, and yet live another.

Understand that the Spirit at home in a Christian does not mean He is in-charge. He can only be in charge, if we let Him. Other than that, He can be there for years, probably all your Christian life without Him ever being in control. He would not overrule your will even though He can. We must yield our will voluntarily and completely to his sway (Colossians 3:9).

Each of us must:"Put off concerning the former conversation the old man, which is corrupt according to the deceitful lusts" (Ephesians 4:22). We must recognize the presence of Jesus on the throne of our heart, and bow in holy reverence to His will. The Holy Spirit must always, at all times and under all circumstances be the boss, and we His bondservants: "The servant is not greater than his Lord" (John 13:16). There is no room for co-equal and co-leadership, not even for head and assistant in the new life.

It may surprise you to know that the closer you move towards God, or move closer to the brightness of His presence, the more you would see how sinful you are. It is like a never ending cleansing, as many sins disappear, many more appear. Sins you never thought existed begin to show up.

But, beloved in the Lord, do not give up, for this is the way it works; it is a revelation of how holy God is. Again it is a reflection of how estranged we are from realities. Abundant help is available, so fight on for the prize of your high calling in Christ (Philippians 3:14).

Unless, from the moment of salvation, we learn to totally surrender our will to the Holy Spirit, we will continue to produce the works of the flesh: "Now the works of the flesh are manifest, which are these; Adultery, fornication, uncleanness, lasciviousness, idolatry, witchcraft, hatred, variance, emulations, wrath, strife, seditions, heresies, envyings, murders, drunkenness, revellings, and such like: of the which I tell you before, as I have also told you in time past, that they which do such things shall not inherit the kingdom of God" (Galatians 5:19-21).

However, if we take our union with Christ seriously, and live daily knowing that we are dead to sin and alive unto God; dead to the Law and married to Christ; dead to the flesh and led by the Spirit, we shall bear much fruit unto God. Growth is guaranteed, if we let the Spirit be our boss, teacher and instructor. We shall bear fruits consistent with our new (divine) nature.

We can all take a practical lesson from Paul in his struggle with indwelling sin in the book of Romans. In chapter 7, Paul is found moaning under the weight of sin which dwells in his flesh: "oh, wretched man that I am! Who shall deliver me from the body of this death" (Romans 7:24). But, in chapter 8, Paul has found an answer to his dare problem. We find him shouting for joy: "Nay, in all these things we are more than conquerors through Him that loved us" (Romans 8:37).

The reason for this turn around and ecstasy is the fact that through Him (Jesus Christ), he has found the much needed strength and power to overcome sin in the flesh through the indwelling Holy Spirit. Hallelujah! Now, he rejoices in God who had not only saved him, but, continues to guarantee his mastery over his enemy (sin) on a daily basis. The Spirit of Christ gives him abundant power to overcome the power of sin in the flesh, the world, and Satan who is the prince of this world.

It is interesting to note, how many times Paul mentions the Holy Spirit in chapter 8 alone; 19 times. Beloved, the only advantage we have as Christians over the lust of the flesh, the lust of the eyes and pride of life (1 John 2:16), is the presence of the indwelling Spirit. God forbid, that any of us should use His grace as a license for sin, so that more grace may abound.

I find it utterly shameful for a Christian who is always at church and yet lives like the devil; in Church on Sundays, but in the service of the devil from Monday to Saturday. No man can faithfully serve two masters (Mathew 6:24). Sin is a principle which is hidden in the flesh of every human being, believer or unbeliever. And for this reason, Paul made the statement: "For I know that in me, that is in my flesh, dwelleth no good thing" (Romans 7:18). This statement is not to say flesh is bad, but simply, one cannot put any confidence in the flesh since it is a host to sin.

Saved by grace through faith, no Christian can make light of the grace of God. God's grace is the more reason each of us must live a holy life. To make practice of sin or occasional excursion into sin is not wise; it means we have not yet learned the cruel and harsh lessons sin taught us while we were held as his prisoners prior to salvation. Only a fool would make mockery of sin. God does not compromise with our sins, He hates them; sin is abhorrent and loathsome. The only wages sin pays to any man is death.

While we are caged in this mortal frame and in the presence of sin, no Christian is and would be entirely free from sinning despite being led by the Spirit. Notwithstanding, living a life without sin as our Lord lived is possible for every Christian; it is possible not to sin through the Holy Spirit.

To make practice of sin is to make light of the second birth; why bathe the pig and array it with white linen just for it to return to the filthy mud? Knowing that it was for our sins Jesus died, it is sheer wickedness to continue in sin after rebirth. Having died once, Jesus lives to die no more. Likewise, we too must reckon ourselves dead once and for all to sin and alive unto God and to righteousness forever. Never should we return to the old lifestyle which killed and made mockery of us.

Born again, we are servants of God and not servants of unrighteousness. We live to serve only one master and to Him we yield our desires, wishes, will. We must exercise to perpetually put our will under the Spirit's control, for God will not over-ride our will.

New life in the Spirit makes no room for the human spirit. Our spirit is one with the Spirit and needs no training to submit or listen to Him (Ephesians 4:24). Instead, our will is that which needs training and to be subjected to the will of the Spirit: "The spirit is willing, but the flesh is weak" is true for every Christian (Mathew 26:41; Mark 14:38). There is no problem with our newly created spirit; he does not need any improvement or development. However, we all must submit our will and incline our ears to the voice of the Spirit:

> **"And thine ears shall hear a word behind thee, saying, This is the way, walk ye in it, when ye turn to the right hand, and when ye turn to the left" (Isaiah 30:21).**

Jesus Christ our Lord calls on every man who has ears to hear (cf. Mark 4:23). Let us incline our hearts to wisdom and understanding, for they are better than platinum and gold. Our spirit has no problem hearing the voice of God, it is a question of whether our will would follow the lead of the Spirit of God; our ears may hear alright, but are we willing?

We are saved by believing and confessing Jesus Christ as our Lord and Savior, which means from the moment of salvation to infinity Jesus, is our Lord. And as Lord, His will is that which must govern our life. He is our Lord in life and in death.

It is rather unfortunate that today, many Christians rely more on their leaders instead of the Holy Spirit. Many preachers are even more popular and better known than the Lord who saved them. Again, many are more inclined to follow the dictates of their denominational leaders instead of the Holy Spirit who dwells in them.

Please, do not get me wrong, I am not saying we should not listen to our leaders; that we should. But, that is only if they themselves are walking in faith; walking and talking in truth. That is, if their lifestyle is consistent to the Word of truth:

"Remember them who have rule over you, who have spoken unto you the word of God: whose faith follow, considering the end of their conversation" (Hebrews 13:7).

We must all accept the fact that all men including Christians are fallible and that no man knows it all. We shall all remain students of the bible and servants of God all the days of our life; ever learning and growing in the Lord. Each individual Christian must learn from our brethren in Thessalonica:

"These were more noble than those in Thessalonica, in that they received the word with all readiness of mind, and searched the scriptures daily, whether those things were so" (Acts 17:11).

They searched the scriptures daily to see whether those things taught by their leaders were in conformity with the written word. Christians today must do the same; we must study the scriptures for ourselves. After every church service, crusade, convention or teaching seminar, we must take the time to do our own research to see if those things taught are true.

Even the times and season in which we live calls urgently that we do so, especially, with so many quack preachers behind the pulpits and others knocking on our doors from day to day. The saying that I have no time is over. Our salvation and future rewards are too important to be entrusted to gainsaying and the hypotheses of ignorant men.

Pertaining to matters of seeming controversy and uncertainty, we must be willing to set aside our own plagiarisms, biases and polarizations, and individually seek the wisdom of God:

"If any of you lacks wisdom, he should ask God, who gives generously to all without finding fault, and it will be given to him" (James 1:5).

When we walk in the Spirit, we need no man to guide and teach us, for the Spirit Himself teaches us all things. It is His duty to teach us what is right and wrong; His responsibility is to guide us into all truth (John 14:26).

Each and every Christian must know we are called to be sons. Sonship can be equated to maturity or coming of age; a point in growth where we are ready to assume family responsibilities as delegated to us. Even though true sonship is in the future, we have already received the Spirit of adoption so that we are able to call God our Father. By the Spirit, we can enter in and take full possession of our spiritual inheritance. We can enjoy our inheritance to the fullest in Christ Jesus.

All that Christ achieved belongs to us: "Every place whereon the soles of your feet shall tread shall be yours" (Deuteronomy 11:24) is also true for every Christian who is led by the Spirit of Jesus Christ. Every Christian lives in a state of 'already and not yet.' Already, we are in our possession; not yet, because we are still waiting for the full and complete possession at the appearing of the Saviour. The greater portion of our inheritance is in the future; yet, through the Spirit, we can begin enjoying them from the moment of salvation. The work of the Spirit is to reveal to the believer all that is ours in Christ, and to make them available for use (John 16:15; 1 Corinthians 2:12).

Born again as spiritual babies by grace through faith, we grow from being children to mature sons as we are led daily by the Spirit of God. A mind change is necessary for growth; the baby mind set must develop into adult mind set. When the mind is allowed to roam freely feasting on anything it can find or allowed to feed on carnal and fleshly things, the result is impeded growth and premature death: "For to be carnally minded is death; but to be spiritually minded is life and peace" (Romans 8:6).

Our old man must be put off, and the new man put on and all has to do with our will and mind. Our will must be handed over, and our mind replaced with the mind of Christ:

"That ye put off concerning the former conversation the old man, which is corrupt according to the deceitful lusts; and be renewed in the spirit of your mind; and that ye put on the new man, which after God is created in righteousness and true holiness" (Ephesians 4:22-24).

When we feed the mind daily with the Word of God, we will be enabled by the Spirit to do those things which are pleasing to God; those things which are expected of the sons of God. We can assume the responsibilities as expected of the sons of God.

The world to me is made up of two types of people; those who have their minds controlled by their sinful nature (their mind set on natural things and care less about the things of God), and those who have their mind controlled by the Spirit (sets their mind after spiritual things or care about the things of God).

These two sets of people have two different world views; have different outcomes in life, and different destinations after this life. One ends in death (1 John 2:17), the other in life everlasting. One produces deadness and emptiness, the other peace and joy in the Holy Spirit (Galatians 6:8).

It is sad, if not tragic, for a Christian to enjoy sinning or wantonly make practice of sin. The effect of sin is like the presence of leprosy or cancer in the body, slowly, it breaks down spiritual immunity and sucks out spiritual energy. Sinful behavior raises the question of genuineness on the part of the Christian (Romans 8:5-17). The strength of sin should not be underestimated:

> "When tempted, no one should say, "God is tempting me." For God cannot be tempted by evil, nor does he tempt anyone; but each one is tempted when, by his own evil desire, he is dragged away and enticed. Then, after desire has conceived, it gives birth to sin; and sin, when it is full-grown, gives birth to death" (James 1:13-15).

The Bible has lots of warning for believers who fall into the pathetic state of willful sinning. Basically, it means two things; it is either the old man is in control or one is a professing Christian. No true child of God enjoys sinning. He cannot sin habitually because the Spirit of God lives in him; he cannot sin because he is born of God (1 John 3:9-10).

God expects all His children to be holy because He is holy (1 Peter 1:18). A disciple of Jesus must show forth evidence of discipleship. We must be prepared to pay any price to avoid sinning against God. "He that saith he abideth in him ought himself also so to walk, even as he walked" (1 John 2:6):

> "For even hereunto were ye called: because Christ also suffered for us, leaving us an example, that ye should follow his steps: Who did no sin, neither was guile found in his mouth: Who, when he was reviled, reviled not again; when he suffered, he threatened not; but committed himself to him that judgeth righteously:
>
> Who his own self bare our sins in his own body on the tree, that we, being dead to sins, should live unto righ-

teousness: by whose stripes ye were healed. For ye were as sheep going astray; but are now returned unto the Shepherd and Bishop of your souls" (1 Peter 2:21-25).

"If ye then be risen with Christ, seek those things which are above, where Christ sitteth on the right hand of God. Set your affection on things above, not on things on the earth. For ye are dead, and your life is hid with Christ in God. When Christ, who is our life, shall appear, then shall ye also appear with him in glory.

Mortify therefore your members which are upon the earth; fornication, uncleanness, inordinate affection, evil concupiscence, and covetousness, which is idolatry: For which things' sake the wrath of God cometh on the children of disobedience: In the which ye also walked some time, when ye lived in them.

But now ye also put off all these; anger, wrath, malice, blasphemy, filthy communication out of your mouth. Lie not one to another, seeing that ye have put off the old man with his deeds; and have put on the new man, which is renewed in knowledge after the image of him that created him" (Colossians 3:1-10).

A Christian is not a sinner but, a saint. When he sins, communication can be disrupted; but, union remains intact. Through the grace of God, the blood of Jesus is available to cleanse us from all sins and to provide immediate restoration to joy and peace with the Father when we admit and confess even when we sin (1 John 1:6-9; 2:15-17).

Your earthly Dad may not speak to you because of your disobedience, but He can never disinherit you. Even if the law of the state or country permits such, it is only on paper; the individual biological family connections remains intact; that no man can ever erase. Such is our union with Christ, we are His blood children; we carry His gene - the Holy Spirit. If you can take it, a Christian may fall on grace but can never fall from grace.

Christians share the same holy family traits with Jesus Christ because they are born of God; they have His Spirit. If we live right, one should be able to say, show me a Christian and I will show you what Jesus is like. God is the Light; we are the reflectors or the little lights. God is Life, we have His life. God is Holy, we have His kind of holiness and the list of similarities goes on. "Both He that sanctifieth and they that are sanctified are all of one: For which cause He is not ashamed to call them brethren" (Hebrews 2:11).

It should not be that because of our character, others won't come to Christ or witness for Christ. The Christian calling is a high calling; a calling that has great responsibility attached. It is a divine calling; it is a transcendent calling. We can enjoy a deeper fellowship with the Spirit, if we take the time to learn from Him, He is more than willing to teach us His ways. We must take the time to sit and learn at His feet; He has more to teach us in a day than all the teachings of men in a lifetime. He is not a teacher, but the teacher. He is the teacher of men. God is not a god; He is 'The God,' the only one true God.

Among the many blessings the Spirit showers upon us, just to name a few are; teaching (John 14:26), bringing to remembrance (John 16:13), bearing witness (John15:26), declaring things to come (John 16:26), glorifying Christ (John 16:14), taking the things that are His and declaring them to the disciple (John 16:14). Other benefits include the following:

1. No condemnation (Romans 8:1)

2. Free from the law of sin and death (Romans 8:2; 10:4)

3. Absence of an attitude of defeat (Romans 8:37)

4. Possibility of life without sin (1 John 3:9)

5. Righteousness of the law fulfilled in us (Romans 8:4)

6. Are not in the flesh but in the Spirit (Romans 8:9)

7. The body is dead because of union with Christ Jesus (Romans 8:10)

8. Joy and peace with God (Romans 5:1; 14:17)

9. The sons of God (Romans 8:14-17)

10. Dead to former lifestyle (Romans 6:11)

11. Sin has no power or control over us (Romans 8:12)

12. Alive in Christ Jesus (Romans 6:11,13)

13. Shall never perish (John 10:28)

14. Transcended lifestyle (1 John 5:11,12)

In conclusion, if we live after the flesh, we shall die: but if we through the Spirit do mortify the deeds of the body, we shall live. This is how the disciples of Jesus lived from the very beginning of the Christian era and the same is true for each of us today. Led by the Spirit, Jesus Christ our Lord, enjoyed victory throughout His earthly life; He breathed, lived, talked, ate, drank, slept, worked, suffered, died, rose again, and ascended into heaven by the Spirit and left us an example to follow (1 Peter 2:21, cf. verse 22). And if this is the way of the master, why should not His servants be in pursuit of the same? After all, Jesus Christ is the believer's life, mind, strength and goal.

Let us learn from our brother Samson (Judges 13-16), incomplete mastery over sin means constant trouble from it afterwards and often defeat by it in the end. Let us beware of ourselves. Victory is inevitable if we follow the way of the Spirit. If we let Him, He shall change every 'I can't' into 'I can': "I can do all things through Christ which strengthens me" (Philippians 4:13). Beloved, let us study the scriptures daily, praying in the Spirit at all times and not neglecting to fellowship with likeminded brethren. Finally, be conscious of His abiding presence.

Chapter Five

No Room for Self

I must admit, the Christian life is as mysterious as the way of an eagle in the air. Can you imagine life without self as the main focus? Such is life as a Christian; it makes no room for self. Self is too small to get attention, but please don't get me wrong, I am not saying self is not important because it is important. Jesus would still have died, even if it was only one person on earth who had sinned. But look at it this way, what is the size of your little village in comparison to the size of the universe? Yet, the universe is incomplete without your village.

Transcended life has God at the center and all others on the circumference. In the kingdom of God, everybody takes care of everybody. Everyone loves God above himself, and everybody loves his neighbor as himself. Wealth and happiness are virtues all Christians share equally. The Christian life is self-less because where self rules, God cannot be and neither can there be faith in God. Self and God are antagonistic. Unregenerate self is selfish; it seeks its own pleasure at the expense of all others and is independent of God.

As creatures of God, we can only find pleasure in the pleasure of our Creator: "For none of us liveth to himself" (cf. Romans

14:7). When God is happy with you, then you can truly enjoy happiness. Life as a Christian is emptied of self because Christ is the Life within the life; He is the center of attention. One cannot be a Christian on his own accord; it has to be given and received and lived as intended.

True Christianity is giving and there cannot be true giving where self is set as a premium.

Let me ask you a few questions. What will you do with self in the following situations? What will you do when all the blessings of God come upon you and overtake you? When God opens the windows of heaven and pours you a blessing that there is no room enough to receive it? What will you do when God makes all His grace abound toward you so that you always have sufficiency in all things? What will you do when God has blessed you exceedingly and abundantly above all that you ask or think, according to the power that works in you? If you are a Christian, then your answers to these questions must matter to you.

The blessings of God are just too much for an individual to spend on self. The sheer weight of such blessings may consume or destroy you. The scope of our calling transcends self and likewise our blessings in Christ. The world is one big palace with both humans and animals feeding at the same dining table. It is, therefore, important for each of us to make sure everybody is okay. There is a reason for us being here (earth), and a reason for the kind of people that we are, and a reason for our current situation whether we see ourselves blessed or not.

Life cannot be created or destroyed by any creature except by the Creator, and neither can life change form. Life is a gift from the Creator to the creature, and this is the reason why each individual human being must come to God for new life without exception. More important to God is the life of a Christian (and I say this without any disrespect to anyone). There is a divine purpose for God waking us up every morning, and likewise, the numbers of years spent on earth. Again, the gifts and talents we each possess are not just for us and our children, but for all.

God has demonstrated in many ways how humanity ought to live as His children; how to relate, one to another. For example, in the beginning of creation, God could have begun the population of the earth by creating billions of people from the onset. But, He, wanting to teach humanity that we are all of one stock, descendants of one blood and one another's keeper, created just one adult couple, and from this couple has come every other human being.

Allow me to digress at this point and share with you a very salient truth: No man on earth is truly blessed until the last of us is blessed. The earth is an inheritance to all human beings, every human being that has lived, living, and would ever live on it. All the blessings, joy, pain, etc., that comes with living in God's lucrative and blissful planet is for all to share. Now, let me share a brief history of why Christian life is devoid of self, why self cannot rule in the second birth, and why no Christian lives to himself.

It all began from eternity past when God the Father gave us this beautiful world and natural life. After man had missed the mark, God, in addition, gave to humanity, spiritual and eternal life by offering the life of His only begotten and beloved Son. As a sin offering for mankind, God gave us His only beloved Son to be the substitute and Savior of every man. All-knowing God had this plan in place even before man was made and before history. God knows all things well in advance before they come into being; nothing takes God by surprise:

"Who verily was foreordained before the foundation of the world, but was manifest in these last times for you" (1 Peter 1:20).

Jesus came to earth from heaven at the time appointed by the Father and as predicted by the prophets. At the right time God honored the promise He made to Adam and Eve and their protégé after they had fallen into sin. Christian life was actually born in history when Jesus died on Calvary cross. God did not force Jesus to come and save humanity; He came voluntarily and vicariously laid down His life for all. He came because He loved us:

"Who gave himself for our sins, that he might deliver us from this present evil world, according to the will of God and our Father" (Galatians 1:4)

Jesus tasted death for every man (Hebrews 2:9). He gave His life as a ransom for all. He took all of our sins upon Himself and gave us all of His righteousness (2 Corinthians 5:17); His life was the sacrifice; His blood was that which was poured on the mercy seat in heaven; He was our atonement (Mark 10:45). He died for every man because He loved every man. The life of every Christian was purchased by His blood (1 Peter 1:18-19):

"Who gave himself for us, that he might redeem us from all iniquity, and purify unto himself a peculiar people, zealous of good works" (Titus 2:14).

Close to the end of His incarnate life, Jesus prayed to the Father for the Holy Spirit. He, therefore, having received the Holy Spirit after His ascension, and having paid the price for our redemption in full, sent Him to earth to help us obtain all that God has graciously given to all men through Him (John 16:7-15).

Again, Jesus did not force the Holy Spirit to come; the Spirit voluntarily offered to come (John 14:17). The Holy Spirit loves us in the same way as the Father and the Son. When the Spirit came, He also gave holy characters (fruits) and Spiritual gifts to men:

"Therefore being by the right hand of God exalted, and having received of the Father the promise of the Holy Ghost, he hath shed forth this, which ye now see and hear" (Acts 2:33).

Now can you see why the Christian life is all about giving? The Father gave, the Son gave, and the Holy Spirit gave. The triune God is a giver and this is the nature of Life as a Christian;

it is about giving, beginning with self. Life begets life:"Forasmuch as ye know that ye were not redeemed with corruptible things, as silver and gold, from your vain conversation received by tradition from your fathers; But with the precious blood of Christ, as a lamb without blemish and without spot (1 Peter 1:18-19):

> **"And this is the record that God has given us eternal life, and this life is in the Son. He that have the Son hath life: and he that have not the Son of God hath not life" (1 John 5:11-12; cf. Romans 6:4).**

I believe from all that has been said so far, that we can create another definition of who is a Christian: A Christian is one who follows the divine example:

> **"For even hereunto are ye called: Because Christ also suffered for us, leaving us an example, that ye should follow his steps" (1 Peter 2:21).**

Each of us is called upon to follow the divine example: "For other foundations can no man lay than that is laid, which is Jesus Christ" (1 Corinthians 3:11). Jesus though was God, emptied Himself (took upon himself our human nature) and humbled Himself (appearing not in splendor) became like one of us, sinful man. As a result God has highly exalted Him and given Him a name, which is above all names.

The same promise of exaltation is reserved before God and the holy angels for each individual Christian. Only if we follow the footsteps of our living Savior and Lord, greater rewards await each of us. If we humble ourselves before God and lay down our lives for Him and his course, we shall possess the heavenly Jerusalem:

> **"He that findeth His life shall lose it: and he that loseth his life for my sake shall find it" (Mathew 10:39).**

If we live a sacrificial life before Him in fear and trembling, we shall be exalted. As already mentioned, Jesus Christ is the

true mind within the mind and strength within the strength of
the Christian:

> "Let this mind be in you which was also in Christ Jesus:
> Who, being in the form of God, thought it robbery to be
> equal with God, but made himself of no reputation, and
> took upon him the form of a servant, and was made in
> the likeness of men:
>
> And being found in fashion as a man, he humbled him-
> self, and became obedient unto death, even the death of
> the cross. Wherefore God also hath highly exalted him,
> and given him a name which is above every name:
>
> That at the name of Jesus every knee should bow, of
> things in heaven and things on earth, and things under
> the earth; and that every tongue should confess that Je-
> sus Christ is Lord, to the glory of God the Father" (Phi-
> lippians 2:5-11).

In response to the gracious acts of God, every Christian is
called upon to voluntarily follow the divine order through self-
denial. Self-humbling is the hallmark of the Christian faith;
Jesus Christ being our supreme example. Though Jesus Christ
is God, He voluntarily condescended to the level of a man, and
not just a man but even lower by becoming a slave and finally
died as a criminal on a wooden cross:

> "I am crucified with Christ: Nevertheless I live; yet not I,
> but Christ liveth in me: and the life which I now live in
> the flesh I live by the faith of the Son of God, who loveth
> me, and gave himself for me" (Galatians 2:20).

Jesus Christ is the foundation on which every one of us is
building on and every man's work shall be tested on the day of
reckoning by fire:

> "And are built upon the foundation of the apostles and
> prophets, Jesus Christ himself being the chief corner
> stone" (1 John 5:11-12).

Every Christian must be totally sold out to Christ and His agenda. The daily life of every Christian is to be lived out through the faith of the Son of God. This means we must depend on the accomplishment of Christ to live our daily Christian life; we must have the same feelings and interests as Christ. His heart must become our heart: "what things were gains to me, those I counted loss for Christ."

"And thou shalt love the Lord thy God with all thy heart, and with all thy soul, and with all thy mind, and with all thy strength: this is the first commandment.

And the second is like, namely this, Thou shalt love thy neighbour as thyself. There is none other commandment greater than these" (Mark 12:30-31).

Each of us rose again with Christ as a creature that is fully God-centered; a new creature that has no self to gratify. Jesus is everything to the Christian (Colossians 3:4): "In Him we live, and move, and have our being" (Acts 17:28). Through Christ we can bear all things:

"I have learned, in whatsoever state I am, therewith to be content. I know both how to be abased, and I know how to be abound" (Philippians 4:11-12).

Union with Christ means oneness with Him; His stripes are for our healing, His death for our offences, his resurrection for our justification, and sanctification and finally, His glorification would be our future glorification: "Christ in me the hope of glory" (Colossians 1:27):

"The way of man is not in himself: it is not in man that walketh to direct his steps" (Jeremiah 10:23).

No Christian lives for and to himself, but unto Him who died and rose again for Him. To place emphases on self is sheer wickedness and there is no room for such in the kingdom of God and of Christ:

"For to me to live is Christ, and to die is gain" (Philippians 1:21).

The resurrected life of a Christian is not his to organize and live as he pleases. Jesus died for all, so that all who may live shall live for Him:

"They which live should not henceforth live unto themselves, but unto him which died for them, and rose again" (2 Corinthians 5:15).

The new life received at regeneration rightfully belongs to God and must be lived for Him. Take note, it is our duty to give it to Him, because He would not take it by force. Once again, our will and agenda must be replaced by His will and agenda:

"And whatsoever ye do in word or deed, do all in the name of the Lord Jesus, giving thanks to God and the Father by him" (Colossians 3:17).

The life of a Christian is gratuitous; to live as a Christian is a man's way of saying thanks to God for all His benefits. Every service or sacrifice that a Christian renders to God and to men in the name of Jesus is, and should be considered gratuitous. For example, when a Christian loves his wife or spouse, gives alms, pays tithes, or worships, it is all gratuitous and must be done in the spirit of gratitude. Equally, when we render love and services to one another, we do them as unto the Lord.

See how God personalizes our response to one another from this quotation: "He that hath pity upon the poor lendeth unto the LORD; and that which he hath given will he pay him again" (Proverbs 19:17). Again, the scriptures declare:

"For none of us liveth to himself, and no man dieth to himself. For whether we live, we live unto the Lord; and whether we die, we die unto the Lord: whether we live therefore, or die, we are the Lord's" (Romans 14:7).

The word 'independence,' is not known in the new life and in the kingdom of God. The only reason the world will not accept theocracy is because it is out of joint with God and His will. The dictionary of heaven contains no words such as self, me, I, independence, or any isms. In Christ, everyone and everything is God dependent. Whatever we do as Christians must be done as to please the Lord and no one else not even ourselves.

For example, a wife is not to please the husband or the husband to please the wife, but the Lord. However, both will find fulfillment in each other as they walk and seek to please the Lord. God should be the love-knot in every relationship whether it's parenthood, marriage, etc. The giver must have His share before the receivers:

> **"Whether therefore ye eat, or drink, or whatsoever ye do, do all to the glory of God" (1 Corinthians 10:31).**

We become like Jesus when we seek to be like Him (Philippians 2:7), but this cannot happen until we first give ourselves to God, then, our sacrifices and offerings. God is not interested in the sacrifice of the wicked (unbeliever) because they are an abomination to Him. God cannot be bribed, and neither can He be fooled by any man's flattery:

> **"Hath the LORD as great delight in burnt offerings and sacrifices, as in obeying the voice of the LORD? Behold, to obey is better than sacrifice, and to hearken than the fat of rams.**
>
> **For rebellion is as the sin of witchcraft, and stubbornness is as iniquity and idolatry. Because thou hast rejected the word of the LORD, he hath also rejected thee from being king" (1 Samuel 15:22-23).**

God is a social being, and so are Christians. We get our own right when we seek the right of others; we feel loved when we love others, and when we forgive others their trespasses against us, then God forgives that which we have committed against Him; we must be willing to do for others what we want God to do for us. The rule of life says, 'what is good for me is good for all.'

What is good for the rich is also good for the poor. For example, if the clothes that the rich wear upon themselves and their children, the cars they drive, the food on their table, etc., are better, then the poor and the needy deserve the same. After all, the same divine hands made us all. Take the teaching of Jesus on forgiveness for a better understanding:

> "Therefore is the kingdom of heaven likened unto a certain king, which would take account of his servants. And when he had begun to reckon, one was brought unto him, which owed him ten thousand talents.
>
> But forasmuch as he had not to pay, his lord commanded him to be sold, and his wife, and children, and all that he had, and payment to be made. The servant therefore fell down, and worshipped him, saying, Lord, have patience with me, and I will pay thee all. Then the lord of that servant was moved with compassion, and loosed him, and forgave him the debt.
>
> But the same servant went out, and found one of his fellowservants, which owed him an hundred pence: and he laid hands on him, and took him by the throat, saying, Pay me that thou owest.
>
> And his fellowservant fell down at his feet, and besought him, saying, Have patience with me, and I will pay thee all. And he would not: but went and cast him into prison, till he should pay the debt. So when his fellowservants saw what was done, they were very sorry, and came and told unto their lord all that was done.
>
> Then his lord, after that he had called him, said unto him, O thou wicked servant, I forgave thee all that debt, because thou desiredst me: Shouldest not thou also have had compassion on thy fellowservant, even as I had pity on thee?" (Mathew 18:23-33).

The rich of this world, believe it or not, cannot be truly happy unless everybody else has a due share, and this applies to rich nations as well. The mass exodus of immigrants from poor countries to the rich countries would never stop unless the poor nations are equally blessed; after all, nobody in the true sense would like to be a friend to poverty. Besides, the resources of the earth are for all to share.

Rich nations can save the enormous money spent each year to curb illegal immigrants by spending to improve the quality of life in the poorest nations; at least give them a descent living. More money or abundant goods does not translate into joy and happiness. One can be very rich and yet unhappy.

Here is another parable as told by our Lord. It is based on a rich young man who came to Jesus seeking life in the kingdom of God:

> "And a certain ruler asked him, saying, Good Master, what shall I do to inherit eternal life? And Jesus said unto him, Why callest thou me good? none is good, save one, that is, God. Thou knowest the commandments, Do not commit adultery, Do not kill, Do not steal, Do not bear false witness, Honour thy father and thy mother. And he said, All these have I kept from my youth up.
>
> Now when Jesus heard these things, he said unto him, Yet lackest thou one thing: sell all that thou hast, and distribute unto the poor, and thou shalt have treasure in heaven: and come, follow me.
>
> And when he heard this, he was very sorrowful: for he was very rich. And when Jesus saw that he was very sorrowful, he said, How hardly shall they that have riches enter into the kingdom of God!
>
> For it is easier for a camel to go through a needle's eye, than for a rich man to enter into the kingdom of God."

And they that heard it said, Who then can be saved? And he said, The things which are impossible with men are possible with God.

Then Peter said, Lo, we have left all, and followed thee. And he said unto them, Verily I say unto you, There is no man that hath left house, or parents, or brethren, or wife, or children, for the kingdom of God's sake, who shall not receive manifold more in this present time, and in the world to come life everlasting" (Luke 18:18-30).

To know the Son of God and be known by Him transcends all earthly glories: "Anyone who layeth up treasure for himself, and is not rich towards God is a fool" (Luke 12:21). To be rich in the sight of God is to seek the good of all men through the Holy Spirit. Self is insatiable and is not subject to change. Self wants it all and wishes that everybody would recognize and come begging.

Christians must seek the good of all men, especially those of the household of faith. We must sincerely love one another; love should be the cause for all charitable works. Love must be the motive for giving; giving without love pays no reward in the kingdom of God; it has no residual value:

"And though I bestow all my goods to feed the poor, and though I give my body to be burned, and have not charity, it profiteth me nothing" (1 Corinthians 13:3).

Love must be the only reason we give. Love does not seek its own. Its own is the Lord; its own is the owner of the universe who seeks the good of all. Love is personified in Christ; love is the rich man (Christ) who came from heaven purposely, to share his riches with all mankind (2 Corinthians 8:9).

Again, love is the longsuffering of God who is still pleading with man to repent and be saved. Where self rules, true love is absent and where true love rules, self is absent:

"Charity suffereth long, and is kind; charity envieth not; charity vaunteth not itself, is not puffed up, doth not

behave itself unseemly, seeketh not her own, is not easily provoked, thinketh no evil; rejoiceth not in iniquity, but rejoiceth in the truth; beareth all things, believeth all things, hopeth all things, endureth all things. Charity never faileth: but whether there be prophecies, they shall fail" (1 Corinthians 13:4-8a)

Love gives 100%. No Christian has contributed towards his salvation. The salvation each of us received by faith is a fully paid for. Spiritually bankrupt, we had nothing to bring; therefore, our heavenly Father gave to each of us 100% of all that is needed to restore us to glory and beyond. Every Christian becomes rich at the expense of Christ.

God takes over a wasted, unprofitable and perishing life, pays off all debts, and then makes it rich by planting us together with His rich Son; thus making us credit worthy (Galatians 4:7; cf. Romans 8:17; Hebrews 1:2; Revelations 5:12). God replaces our poor and unworthy life with the rich life of His worthy Son:

"For ye know the grace of our Lord Jesus Christ, that, though he was rich, yet for your sakes he became poor, that ye through his poverty might be rich" (2 Corinthians 8:9).

Now, armed with all this information, answer for yourself these questions: Is it possible for a Christian who is a recipient of such gracious generosity to withhold from God? Can Christians withhold from those who need their help or withhold from the less fortunate? Can any of us hold tight to what has been freely given and received?

I tell you, the answer to all of the above is no. It is the secondary duty of every Christian to share what we have with all who have not. This may sound difficult, but to whom much is given, much is required. The glory of Love is that love never ceases. God who gave the world and His Son and His Spirit is still giving.

Every day, plants, animals, and humans receive abundant blessings of life and sustenance from him: "He that spared not his own Son, but delivered him up for us all, how shall he not with him also freely give us all things?" (Romans 8:32). One cannot be a true disciple of Jesus and hold tenaciously to family, spouse, children, self, and personal effects.

Each individual Christian must be prepared to forsake all and to suffer for His name sake (Luke 14:24). It is expected that every man aspire to be like Jesus Christ self-sacrificing and self-humbling:

> "That ye may be the children of your Father which is in heaven: for He maketh His sun to rise on the evil and on the good, and sendeth rain on the just and on the unjust" (Mathew 5:45).

The kindergarten of Christianity begins with knowing your why: Why you believe; why you are a Christian; and why God chose you. Further, you must know why God did what he did for you and why He was willing to pay such a hefty price for your freedom. There is only one answer to all of these questions: God created us in order that we may live happily together with Him, and it is for this reason Jesus died to bring us back to God:

> "For Christ also hath once suffered for sins, the just for the unjust, that he might bring us to God, being put to death in the flesh, but quickened by the Spirit" (1 Peter 3:18).

> "And walk in love, as Christ also hath loved us, and hath given himself for us an offering and a sacrifice to God for a sweetsmelling savior" (Ephesians 5:2).

Who knows why many prayers are not answered; maybe it is because they are full of self, or full of I or me and self. We ask for things to consume with the flesh and not for His honor and glory. Christians are channels of blessings; we receive from God and pass it on to others. Then, they who receive also pass it on to others and the chain of giving continues.

On the reverse, praise and adoration pours from the lips of the last recipient to the first; multiples of praises rise to the throne room of grace through giving and receiving. God rejoices, and the circle continues. In addition, the joy of all multiplies because everyone has the opportunity of showing gratitude to God.

We maintain a constant state of fullness when we come to know the love of Christ and the blessings of giving. Apart from maintaining a state of fullness, we become blessed with constant overflow (Ephesians 3:19-20; cf.1:23). Overflow makes up for the shortage in others, till we all come to a state of fullness (2 Kings 4:6; Mathew 15:37).

There are so many needs in the world and in the body of Christ; there are too many people who need our help daily. Overflow is what supplies the need of others while maintaining fullness without ourselves running short (3 John 2):

"Hereby perceive we the love of God, because he laid down his life for us: and we ought to lay down our lives for the brethren" (1John 3:16).

Jesus once told the parable of a man who was so blessed that instead of being an imitator of God by being a cheerful giver, decided to keep all to himself:

"And he spake a parable unto them, saying, The ground of a certain rich man brought forth plentifully: And he thought within himself, saying, what shall I do, because I have no room where to bestow my fruits?

And he said, this will I do: I will pull down my barns, and build greater; and there will I bestow all my fruits and my goods. And I will say to my soul, Soul, thou hast much goods laid up for many years; take thine ease, eat, drink, and be merry.

But God said unto him, Thou fool, this night thy soul shall be required of thee: then whose shall those things be, which thou hast provided? So is he that layeth up treasure for himself, and is not rich toward God" (Luke 12:16-21).

Greedy self is another reason we have a world that is opposed to the will of God. The worldly man says what is mine is mine, but the Christian says what is mine is yours. Where the Spirit rules, love and submissiveness rule:

"But God forbid that I should glory, save in the cross of our Lord Jesus Christ, by whom the world is crucified unto me, and I unto the world" (Galatians 6:14).

Think of this, what profit is it to you to have billions of earthly goods while your fellow men are dying from lack of basic human needs:

"For whosoever will save his life shall lose it: and whosoever will lose his life for my sake shall find it" (Mathew 16:24).

Our heavenly Father cares much about the right of all to descent life because there is enough for all. Human life is far more precious than goods and animals. Huge sums of money spent on war machines can be spent to improve the quality of life and existence of all men. The well-being of all mankind is the duty of all:

"Are not five sparrows sold for two farthings, and not one of them is forgotten before God? But even the very hairs of your head are all numbered. Fear not therefore: ye are of more value than many sparrows" (Luke 12:6-7).

We must not forget, for Jesus warned us against the increase of worldly goods:

"Lay not up for yourselves treasures upon earth, where moth and rust doth corrupt, and where thieves break through and steal: But lay up for yourselves treasures in

heaven, where neither moth nor rust doth corrupt, and where thieves do not break through nor steal: For where your treasure is, there will your heart be also" (Mathew 6:19-21).

There is no place for self-rule in the new man and the new life: "For I was alive without the law once: but when the commandment came, sin revived, and I died" (Romans 7:9). "For I through the law am dead to the law, that I might live unto God" (Galatians 2:21).

What comes to mind first thing in the morning and last before bed time? What occupies the mind throughout the day determines whether self or Spirit is ruling. True life is that which is lived under the rule of God.

Very often, you hear, especially church leaders make the following statements; we want to build a large church; we want to have branches all over the world; we want to organize a large choir; we want to buy forty acres of land for the Lord, we want to have a radio or television ministry to spread the Gospel, etc. To be honest, none of these ventures are bad in themselves.

But, the question each of us must ask before taking any of these ventures in the name of God is whether any of it is for the glory of God. Yes, they are done in the name of Jesus, but who actually gets the glory and who are the beneficiaries?

I believe the starting question for any work done in God's name is a critical examination of our conscience and motive. We must make sure that pure necessity, hardship, and self aggrandizement is not the driving force. For example, to enter the pastoral calling because of retirement, unemployment, failures, misfortune, or even fame and riches may not be a smart idea.

Each of us must make it a responsibility to ask ourselves: Has God really asked me to do what I am doing in His name, or am I by myself doing them for Him? Are we trying to win His favor by self-effort or trying to help Him accomplish His purpose? No work is worth doing for God if He has not asked us to do it.

The tragedy with some of our Church leaders is that they fail to acknowledge that God honors and protects His name and that signs and wonders are not necessarily approval of character or works. Huge crusades, large congregations, and many people saved are not always signs of approval and acceptances of method used and or even work done.

Sometimes, we put God in a box; we make Him defend His name unwillingly. To be honest, any unbeliever who gathers people in the name of Jesus and preaches the word even out of spite, pretence or greed may see great and positive results. In the same vein, it may be possible for a preacher to share his bed with a prostitute on Saturday night, and yet, see many souls converted on the alter Sunday morning.

Many of the mighty moves of God are permitted because God protects His Holy name and glory and not because He approves the lifestyle, motives, and the means by which these works are done in His name:

"For mine own sake, even for mine own sake, will I do it: for how should my name be polluted? and I will not give my glory unto another" (Isaiah 48:11).

Furthermore, sad to mention is that things acquired in the name of God in many cases end up becoming personal or family property. They are often wasted, laid to waist, or even used for ungodly purposes. Huge sums of money that could have been used for Gospel outreach are used on custom made church buildings, church decorations, and top notch technology.

Others use it for expensive clothing, cars, and mansions. Many who are paid handsomely engage in fanciful lifestyles. Please, understand that I am not saying these things are bad in themselves; after all, the laborer deceives his wages. However, the question we must all ask is how shall all this play for us on the judgment day or at the judgment seat of Christ? Will He say well done or you wicked, get away from me?

Christians have received a holy calling; the way of life is the way of holiness without which no man shall see the Lord. It is about time, we all re-examine our motives and consciences for the day of the Lord is fast approaching. We have a God-given responsibility to seek the rights and welfare of all men and to preach the Gospel to all men. There is nothing like, what is in there for me in the kingdom of God because, all belongs to Him:

"If any man will do his will, he shall know of the doctrine, whether it be of God, or whether I speak of myself. He that speaketh of himself seeketh his own glory: but he that seeketh his glory that sent him, the same is true, and no unrighteousness is in him" (James 4:5).

God has promised to take care of the needs of every man, so that every man can take care of the kingdom business:"Therefore take no thought, saying, what shall we eat? or, What shall we drink? or, Wherewithal shall we be clothed? (For after all these things do the Gentiles seek) for your heavenly Father knoweth that ye have need of all these things" (Mathew 6:31-32).

If we have the feelings of Christ, then we shall have the same interest as Christ; His concerns become our supreme concern:

"Christ shall be magnified in my body, whether it be life, or by death" (Mathew 6:31-32).

We can summarize all that has been said so far by concluding, life as a Christian began with God giving us life through His Son. Jesus purchased life for every man by His voluntary and vicarious death on the cross of Calvary. That which was purchased was brought down to man by the voluntary coming of the Holy Spirit. Trinity is the source of all giving.

Christians are imitators of God by first giving themselves to God. Life as a Christian is self-humbling and self-sacrificing. Here is the supreme example. "Let this mind be in you which was also in Christ." It is giving from start to finish. Everybody in the family of God gives, starting from the Father to the least in His kingdom. True giving is emptied of self; it is full of love. Where self rules, the Spirit is either silenced or absent because self and the Spirit cannot co-exist and co-rule.

From the moment of rebirth, the Holy Spirit begins the work of Christ by seeking to reach others through us. He seeks the welfare, salvation, and the dignity of men through us: "According to my earnest expectation and my hope, that in nothing I shall be ashamed, but that with all boldness, as always, so now also Christ shall be magnified in my body, whether it be by life, or by death" (Philippians 1:20).

Chapter Six

LIBERTY IN THE SPIRIT

 Liberty (freedom) is the perfect description of life in the Spirit. Liberty is the birth right of every Christian. He that is born of God is the Lord's freed man; the state into which every believer is born and lives. Even in this life, Christians through the Spirit can live the blissful life of liberty. Without the law to condemn and self to gratify, every Christian is forever free to live as God intended.

The highest blessing that can be bestowed on any human being is to be freed from sin, the power of sin and the wages of sin:

"Blessed is the man unto whom the LORD imputeth not iniquity, and in whose spirit there is no guile" (Psalm 32:2).

No man can enjoy true freedom unless he is freed from the clutches of sin. Joy and happiness become a possession of the soul, only when the heart is beamed with light from above and the thick darkness that veils the soul is removed. Sin is a potent evil that wages war against the human soul; it offers no rest to the soul.

Liberty is achieved only when there is peace and fellowship between the Creator and the creature between God and man.

Liberty for man is not achievable by self effort and neither can it be gained politically. Let me put it bluntly, any man who wants freedom must be emancipated by Jesus Christ.

Liberty is a gift from God and can only be received gratuitously; it is unmerited. To be justified is the beginning of freedom. He that is freed by God lives to sin no more and by that every Christian is a free man. Jesus characterized his mission by quoting the prophet Isaiah:

> "The Spirit of the Lord is on me, because he has anointed me to preach good news to the poor. He has sent me to proclaim freedom for the prisoners and recovery of sight for the blind, to release the oppressed" (Luke 4:18).

Jesus Christ came to set the captive free, so that we may be free to serve God in holy reverence, righteousness and true holiness. When Jesus said: "Greater things shall you do," He was not just referring to miracle works, but also to the quality of liberty that is already our possession in Christ:

> "If the Son therefore shall make you free, ye shall be free indeed" (John 8:36).

Men fear death and not sin, but they forget that sin is death (the wages of sin is death). Sin is a principle that produces death in every man; it can only be destroyed by the regenerative power of the Holy Spirit. He that is dead in Christ is freed from sin and death; he lives not only to sin no more but to die no more:

> "My sheep hear my voice, and I know them and they follow me: And I give them eternal life; and they shall never perish, neither shall they any man pluck them out of my hand. My Father, which gave them to me, is greater than all; and no man is able to pluck them out of my Father's hand" (John 10:27-29).

> "Because through Christ Jesus the law of the Spirit of life set me free from the law of sin and death" (Romans 8:2).

There is freedom in not having to answer to any man, but God. Men can sometimes be cruel and savage. There is a beast-like nature in every man. King David said, he would rather that God punish him than to fall into the hands of man and he was right (2 Samuel 24:14). Men sometimes would:

"Bind heavy burdens and grievous to be borne, and lay them on men's shoulders; but they themselves will not move them with one of their fingers" (Mathew 23:4).

"Now therefore why tempt ye God, to put a yoke upon the neck of the disciples, which neither our fathers nor we were able to bear Hear what the Spirit says would come forth in these last days" (Acts 15:10).

Born from above, Christians are by nature law abiding. They live by orders and standards which transcend any rule, legislation, and standards of men. They live by the standards and orders of heaven. What may not be sin in the eyes of men may be sin in the sight of God. The only time a Christian may be looked upon as breaking the law of the state or land is when such law is in conflict with the law of God:

"Ye have heard that it was said by them of old time, Thou shalt not commit adultery: But I say unto you, that whosoever looketh on a woman to lust after her hath committed adultery with her already in his heart.

And if thy right eye offend thee, pluck it out, and cast it from thee: for it is profitable for thee that one of thy members should perish, and not that thy whole body should be cast into hell" (Mathew 5:27-29).

"There is one lawgiver, who is able to save and to destroy: who art thou that judgest another?" (James 4:12). The life of every Christian is lived at the dictate of the Holy One, and as a result they can't obey any law that is in conflict with their new nature (1 Corinthians 10:26):"For the earth is the Lord's, and the fullness thereof."

As pilgrims and strangers on earth, Christians have very little attachment to earthly lifestyle (1 Peter 2:11). Their obedience, devotion, reverence, and fear is to God and God only. They fear no man, and nothing can by any means hurt them:

"And fear not them which kill the body, but are not able to kill the soul: but rather fear him which is able to destroy both soul and body in hell" (Mathew 10:28; Luke 12:4).

Irrespective of earthly status and condition, Christians are free from all that binds men of natural descent (1 Corinthians 7:23). For example, they are free from the deceitfulness of riches, vanity, and lust. Earthly glories and fame mean very little to them, for they look forward to receiving incorruptible crowns on the day of the Lord. Every Christian looks forward to a new heaven and a new earth. They seek a city which hath foundations, whose builder and maker is God (Hebrews 11:10). They look forward to been clothed with that which is not made with human hands, ready and reserved heaven for them (2 Corinthians 5:1).

Even though true freedom for each of us is in the future, Christians through the indwelling Spirit can begin to enjoy every bit of it, even now:

"Now the Lord is that Spirit: and where the Spirit of the Lord is, there is liberty" (2 Corinthians 3:17).

Life in the Spirit is a roller coaster; it is like the eagle enjoying the heavy storms. In fact, Christians ought to be happy every single day of the earthly existence. Life on earth is a vacation, and nothing must be allowed to take the fun and joy away. Though, there is a missionary agenda attached to our earthly stay, it is still full of fun. The Lord is the Spirit or the Holy Spirit is Lord, and where the Spirit of the Lord is, there is liberty.

Christian liberty is rooted in the grace of God. God's grace is rich and free for all. There is a deep distinction between grace and the law. Law is for the natural man and grace for the spiritual man (Christian). Law signifies restrictions; there is no law in liberty. The Old Covenant laws, for example, engendered to bondage to all those who were under its administration. Anyone born under the old covenant was considered a child of slavery, because of the law which was attached. But, children born under the new covenant, the covenant of grace, are children of freedom.

This distinction together with others has been the cause of persecution of Christians since her birth. Today, many Christians are being persecuted because of their hard stand for the truth of God's Word. For outsiders, Christians don't seem to fit properly into the life pattern and the mindset of this world. In the eyes of the world, Christians are odd. Sometimes old friends think of it strange that we no longer join them in their earthly sensual and fleshly rioting and debauchery:

"For the time past of our life may suffice us to have wrought the will of the Gentiles, when we walked in lasciviousness, lusts, excess of wine, revellings, banquetings, and abominable idolatries:

Wherein they think it strange that ye run not with them to the same excess of riot, speaking evil of you" (1 Peter 4:3-4).

———————————————

"If ye were of the world, the world would love his own: but because ye are not of the world, but I have chosen you out of the world, therefore the world hateth you" (John 15:19).

A symbolic example of the struggle between the flesh and the Spirit can be found in the unfriendly feud between Isaac and Ishmael, the two sons of Abraham. I pick these two because their descendants are still fighting with each other to this hour.

Isaac was a man born after the Spirit, born of a free woman (legitimate wife), and born out of the promise of God; his birth was a miracle or supernatural. He is considered the legitimate son of Abraham. Chosen by God, he was the man through whom the Messianic promise was to be fulfilled. Isaac allegorically represents the new covenant (the covenant of grace), and the Jerusalem which is above.

Ishmael, the oldest son of Abraham, on the other hand, was a man born after the flesh through unbelief (born of a bond maid), and the one who persecuted Isaac, the child of promise. Ishmael allegorically represents Mount Sinai in Arabia, the official birth place of the Old Covenant (the law of bondage), subject to the Jerusalem above. Ishmael, when he was a young lad was caught mocking Isaac and, therefore, driven away together with his mother (Genesis 21:8ff).

These early conflicts between these two sons were later aggravated by the conflict between Jacob and Esau. Esau sold his birthright to Isaac, yet wanted the blessings due only to the first born. This ancient conflict has descended through the generations and is very much alive in the current Arab-Israel tensions (Genesis 27:40ff).

Furthermore, the scripture is clear that Christians like Isaac are born of the Spirit; they are children of promise. This scripture is not saying Christians descended from Isaac because we did not. Regenerates are children of promise and are therefore legitimate sons of God. The world does not know us because even though Christians are in the world they are not of the world (John 17:14-15):

"Now we, brethren, as Isaac was, are the children of promise. But as then he that was born after the flesh persecuted him that was born after the Spirit, even so it is now. Nevertheless what saith the scripture? Cast out the bondwoman and her son: for the son of the bondwoman shall not be heir with the son of the freewoman. So then, brethren, we are not children of the bondwoman, but of the free" (Galatians 4:28-31).

Grace flows from the love of God. There is no fear in love: "Perfect love casteth out fear (1 John 4:18). We love because we have the love of God in our hearts and because He first loved us. Both grace and love embodies a good deed done without expectation of returned favor; Christians serve God wholeheartedly and with no fear of punishment. We hate to sin, not for fear of punishment, but because we love God sincerely. We are not debtors to sin, but righteousness.

For example, when Christians give offering and tithes, they do so in the newness of spirit. We give as the Spirit would have it or direct, without any fear of judgment or curse. Malachi 3:10 does not work under the dispensation of grace. We give because we love God; ours is an offering of thanksgiving - thanksgiving for what He has already done and that which He is yet to do. We know He will bless us with more when we do His will; when we obey His commandment.

The Law, be that of God or the state, is not for the righteous man, but for the unrighteous: "Because the law worketh wrath: for where no law is, there is no transgression (Romans 4:15). Sin is lawlessness. "For as many as are of the works of the law are under the curse: for it is written, Cursed is everyone that continueth not in all things which are written in the book of the law to do them" (Galatians 3:10).

Real liberty is the possession of the truth as cometh from God. Truth has an unalterable validity or stability, and therefore, must be accepted by all men. Christians are free because they have the truth; they are indwelt by the Spirit of truth. Knowledge of the truth sets men free. Truth when believed and practiced becomes a state - a state of freedom:

"And ye shall know the truth, and the truth shall make you free" (John 8:32).

"By whom also we have access by faith into this grace wherein we stand, and rejoice in hope of the glory of God" (Romans 5:2; cf. Romans 3:20).

The work of the Spirit is to lead unbelievers to Jesus who is the embodiment and revelation of the truth (1 John 5:20; cf. 14:6). The Spirit teaches Christians the truth about Himself, the Father and the Son (John 15:26; 1 John 5:6). Truth brings a release - a release from servitude to sinful lust, ignorance, fear and unbelief (John 8:32; Romans 1:21; 6:16; Ephesians 4:18).

Jesus came preaching and teaching the way of God in truth (Mark 12:14) for the will of God is that all men would know and come to the knowledge of the truth so that they might be set free (1 Timothy 2:4).

Many people dream of a state of freedom, but their conception and understanding of freedom is very sketchy and neither do they know how or where to find it. True freedom can only be found in the Gospel; the Gospel of Jesus Christ is the highway to freedom. Truth is personified in His person.

Liberty as a gift from God can only be found in Him. Now, since all men are in need of freedom, all must go to Jesus to get freedom. The only true freedom that exists, and that which man needs, is that which God alone provides. God Himself is man's freedom. Freedom in God is man's utmost utopia.

Let me share with you some illusions about true freedom. Real freedom is not the power to do as one pleases. It is not freedom from physical restraint. It is not freedom from arbitrary or despotic control. It is not the positive enjoyment of various social, political, or economic rights and privileges. It is not found in nature. It is not found in revealed religion, and of course, not in man. It is not the power of choice; for example, having more money and achieving the highest pinnacle of education and fame cannot produce freedom.

Adam and Eve, the wealthiest couple that ever lived, had freedom in a way no human being would ever know, apart from Jesus; yet, when they chose what was pleasing to them in contradistinction to the will of God; they immediately fell into bondage and died slaves to sin and Satan. As you already know, it is primarily the result of their action that we all die.

Again, let me briefly show you what can be considered as real freedom (liberty). Real freedom is the freedom to do that which is right, pure, and good in the sight of God and men. It is the freedom of not being able to sin and being filled with the fullness of Christ. Freedom for every man depends upon obedience to divine command.

Man was made and formed as a free moral being; he was created morally perfect and righteous (Ecclesiastes 7:29). He was created a king with the earth as his palace, the lower creatures as his servants, and the fruits and vegetables as food on his table. He lost his liberty and became a slave only when he failed his probation and broke the only divine prohibition:

"And the LORD God commanded the man, saying, Of every tree of the garden thou mayest freely eat: But of the tree of the knowledge of good and evil, thou shalt not eat of it: for in the day that thou eatest thereof thou shalt surely die" (Genesis 2:17)

Adam and his wife Eve had everything they needed in abundance; theirs was provision in perfection and profusion. Their disobedience was therefore inexcusable; they were culpable for their action. They acted in pure unbelief. Unbelief can be described as the sin of all sins - the great enemy of mankind. Whatsoever is not of faith is sin (Romans 14:23), and sinners cannot find the rest or enjoy the freedom God gives (Isaiah 28:12; 57:20):

"Know ye not, that to whom ye yield yourselves servants to obey, his servants ye are to whom ye obey; whether of sin unto death, or of obedience unto righteousness?" (Romans 6:16).

Lack of faith in God or unbelief underscores all the sins committed by mankind. Every action of man is piloted either by belief or unbelief of the divine will. Belief and unbelief are mutually exclusive and diametrically opposed to each other. Belief in God leads to life; unbelief leads to death. Death, poverty, sickness and disease, racial discrimination, religious error, classification among men and all human vice exist as a result of the fall (the fall of man), and as a consequence of unbelief (Genesis 3).

Jesus Christ is the believer's rest. The law came by Moses, but grace and peace came by Jesus Christ. Liberty and grace are inseparable; grace is the sea, and liberty the bedrock. In Christ, he who is born of God is born into true freedom because he cannot sin (1 John 3:9). The purpose of God in Christ is to give all His adopted sons rest (Mathew 11:28-30):

> **"There remaineth therefore a rest to the people of God. For he that is entered into his rest, he also hath ceased from his own works, as God did from his. Let us labour therefore to enter into that rest, lest any man fall after the same example of unbelief" (Hebrews 4:9-11).**

Christ the great liberator sets anyone free who comes to God through Him by faith:

> **"For the law of the Spirit of life in Christ Jesus hath made me free from the law of sin and death. For what the law could not do, in that it was weak through the flesh, God sending his own Son in the likeness of sinful flesh, and for sin, condemned sin in the flesh" (Romans 8:2-3).**

In Christ, customs, traditions, religions and religious rites (e.g., circumcision), Judaism, heathenism, paganism and all isms become things of the past (Hebrews 2:15); behold all things have become new. Strict adherence to Sabbaths, days, moons and seasons have no meaning whatsoever. They are all considered bondages from which Christ has come to set man free:

> **"Know ye not, brethren, (for I speak to them that know the law,) how that the law hath dominion over a man as long as he liveth? For the woman which hath an husband is bound by the law to her husband so long as he liveth; but if the husband be dead, she is loosed from the law of her husband.**

So then if, while her husband liveth, she be married to another man, she shall be called an adulteress: but if her husband be dead, she is free from that law; so that she is no adulteress, though she be married to another man.

Wherefore, my brethren, ye also are become dead to the law by the body of Christ; that ye should be married to another, even to him who is raised from the dead, that we should bring forth fruit unto God.

For when we were in the flesh, the motions of sins, which were by the law, did work in our members to bring forth fruit unto death. But now we are delivered from the law, that being dead wherein we were held; that we should serve in newness of spirit, and not in the oldness of the letter" (Romans 7:1-6).

Many times, Christians for fear of persecution are found to be compromisers, but this ought not to be. We must fear God rather than men: "And fear not them which kill the body, but are not able to kill the soul: but rather fear him which is able to destroy both soul and body in hell" (Mathew 10:28). We must be strong, uncompromising, unyielding and unmovable in the liberty, which has been costly purchased for us in Christ:

"Stand fast therefore in the liberty wherewith Christ hath made us free, and be not entangled again with the yoke of bondage. Behold, I Paul say unto you, that if ye be circumcised, Christ shall profit you nothing.

For I testify again to every man that is circumcised, that he is a debtor to do the whole law. Christ is become of no effect unto you, whosoever of you are justified by the law; ye are fallen from grace.

For we through the Spirit wait for the hope of righteousness by faith. For in Jesus Christ neither circumcision availeth any thing, nor uncircumcision; but faith which worketh by love" (Galatians 5:1-6).

Further, Christians are sometimes made to feel guilty for no apparent reasons. People who have very little or no knowledge of the Christian faith work hard to dilute, belittle or destroy the Christian doctrine. Unable to destroy the church from the outside, others have secretly crept in to destroy from within:

> **"And that because of false brethren unawares brought in, who came in privily to spy out our liberty which we have in Christ Jesus, that they might bring us into bondage"** (Galatians 2:4).

From the pulpit, Christians are told to do so many things which are purported to be scriptural and coming from God. Instead, many are doctrines of men and demons. The scriptures are intentionally or unintentionally misapplied and manipulated for man's benefit. We wish all those who call themselves men and women of God, pastors, or preachers be genuine and truly called of God. Unfortunately, this is not the case.

There are many faithful ministers of God. There are also many false, self-proclaimed, institutionally ordained ministers, and false leaders within the Church. The scriptures carry enough warnings for every Christian:

> **"Then the LORD said unto me, The prophets prophesy lies in my name: I sent them not, neither have I commanded them, neither spake unto them: they prophesy unto you a false vision and divination, and a thing of nought, and the deceit of their heart"** (Jeremiah 14:14)

> **"Behold, I am against them that prophesy false dreams, saith the LORD, and do tell them, and cause my people to err by their lies, and by their lightness; yet I sent them not, nor commanded them: therefore they shall not profit this people at all, saith the LORD"** (Jeremiah 23:32).

"For they prophesy falsely unto you in my name: I have not sent them, saith the LORD" (Jeremiah 29:9).

"For there shall arise false Christs, and false prophets, and shall shew great signs and wonders; insomuch that, if it were possible, they shall deceive the very elect" (Mathew 24:24).

"But there were false prophets also among the people, even as there shall be false teachers among you, who privily shall bring in damnable heresies, even denying the Lord that bought them, and bring upon themselves swift destruction" (2 Peter 2:1).

"Beloved, believe not every spirit, but try the spirits whether they are of God: because many false prophets are gone out into the world" (1 John 4:1).

Just as leaders seek to teach members to be ready for the judgment seat of Christ, likewise, church members must equally help church leaders to be good stewards for the day of the Lord is at hand:

"But I keep my body, and bring it into subjection: lest by any means, when I have preached to others, I myself should be castaway" (1 Corinthians 10:27).

The simplicity of the Gospel must not be compromised; the Christian faith must be guarded and maintained by all believers. Godly contentment is a great gain. Christians are freed from working as a means of pleasing God. We depend on the Holy Spirit through the faith of Christ to do the works of God. This means we work only on the impulse and strength of the Spirit (Galatians 5:16-18). To believe is to work (Mark 9:23). Even though Christians are in the world, they are an enigma to the world as already mentioned (1 John 3:1):

> **"For whatsoever is born of God overcometh the world: and this is the victory that overcometh the world, even our faith. Who is he that overcometh the world, but he that believeth that Jesus is the Son of God?" (1 John 5:4-5).**

Now, here is my advice. Relying on the strength of the Spirit: Let each man denounce anything that rises against the knowledge and will of God; "renounce the hidden things of dishonesty, not walking in craftiness, nor handling the word of God deceitfully but by manifestation of the truth commending ourselves to every man's conscience in the sight of God" (2 Corinthians 4:2). We must do away with old pagan practices for they are an abomination to the Lord:

> **"Howbeit then, when ye knew not God, ye did service unto them which by nature are no gods. But now, after that ye have known God, or rather are known of God, how turn ye again to the weak and beggarly elements, whereunto ye desire again to be in bondage? Ye observe days, and months, and times, and years" (Galatians 4:9-10).**

> **"Wherefore if ye be dead with Christ from the rudiments of the world, why, as though living in the world, are ye subject to ordinances, (touch not; taste not; handle not; which all are to perish with the using) after the commandments and doctrines of men?" (Colossians 2:20-22).**

Christians must stand firm on the truth and the liberty of the Gospel of grace, and not be entangled again with the yoke of the traditions of men: "Now therefore why tempt ye God, to put a yoke upon the neck of the disciples, which neither our fathers nor we were able to bear; here what the Spirit says would come forth in these last days" (Acts 15:10); such as what to eat or not, wear and not wear and many others. Doctrines have their source in man and will all end with man:

"Now the Spirit speaketh expressly, that in the latter times some shall depart from the faith, giving heed to seducing spirits, and doctrines of devils; speaking lies in hypocrisy; having their conscience seared with a hot iron;

Forbidding to marry, and commanding to abstain from meats, which God hath created to be received with thanksgiving of them which believe and know the truth.

For every creature of God is good, and nothing to be refused, if it be received with thanksgiving: For it is sanctified by the word of God and prayer" (1 Timothy 4:1-5).

Again, let us follow the examples of our Elders: "And many that believed came, and confessed, and shewed their deeds. Many of them also, which used curious arts brought their books together, and burned them before all men: and they counted the price of them, and found it fifty thousand pieces of silver" (Acts 19:18-19). Unbelievers do care much about the things of this world, living constantly in fear of death and judgment, but we believers follow the things of the Spirit. The spirit in us is not that of bondage, but of sonship:

"For ye have not received the spirit of bondage again to fear; but ye have received the Spirit of adoption, whereby we cry, Abba, Father" (Romans 8:15).

"For God hath not given us the spirit of fear; but of power, and of love, and of a sound mind" (2 Timothy 1:7).

The church as a living organism means individual Christians are not only directly connected to the Christ, but have access to the Father by the Holy Spirit. Christ is our access to God and the only mediator between man and God. Through His spirit, we can communicate with the Father any where at any time.

Christians do not need special candles, garments, special ornaments and incense to worship or pray to God (Romans

5:2; Ephesians 2:18; 3:12); and neither do we need special bath or cleansing water and oil to make us spiritually clean (Mathew 18:20). Every Christian is already clean by the Word and by the Holy Spirit. God, through the blood of Jesus has them clean forever (Hebrews 9:12).

Satan would not hesitate to shame any of us if we let him or if we fail to heed scriptural warnings (Romans 2:24). We must hold on to our liberty in Christ tenaciously. Leaders and non-leaders of the faith must guard against our common enemy Satan, who works by sin. The call to ministry and leadership is no immunity from moral decadence and neither would such a call automatically erase sin from any Christian. Being called into the ministry is no immunity from sin.

If a Christian makes practice of sin his sinning would not go away because he has been called into ministry. A minister of the Gospel like every other Christian must trust the indwelling Spirit to conform him into the image and likeness of God on a daily basis, without which his calling would be dwarfed and marred by sin, shame, and reproach. I say this as a fellow minister of the Gospel of Christ; if Satan can get the leader, the flock would not be spared. He would scatter the sheep.

Leaders and non-leaders alike must pray, read, and study the Bible for maturity and a deepening walk with God, and not just for the work of the ministry (1 Peter 1:13-25). We must all inclusively, cooperate with the Holy Spirit to work on our character. We must individually develop private enhancement programs and spiritual exercises; times when we seek God personally. Each individual must have a desire for holiness and a cry to be like Jesus - this is real liberty:

"This know also, that in the last days perilous times shall come. For men shall be lovers of their own selves, covetous, boasters, proud, blasphemers, disobedient to parents, unthankful, unholy, without natural affection, trucebreakers, false accusers, incontinent, fierce, despisers of those that are good, traitors, heady, highminded, lovers of pleasures more than lovers of God;

Having a form of godliness, but denying the power thereof: from such turn away. For of this sort are they which creep into houses, and lead captive silly women laden with sins, led away with divers lusts.

Ever learning, and never able to come to the knowledge of the truth. Now as Jannes and Jambres withstood Moses, so do these also resist the truth: men of corrupt minds, reprobate concerning the faith. But they shall proceed no further: for their folly shall be manifest unto all men, as their's also was" (2 Timothy 3:1-9).

The way some local church organizations are funded today places many Christians under the spirit of bondage. Unfortunately, many resort to unholy acts; some engage in very questionable methods. Even though such practices are unworthy and dishonoring to the Lord, it seems these ministers want to assert that the end justifies the means. Can Christians rob the bank to promote the work of God?

I believe a critical question Church leaders and congregations must address in our day is, should the Church continue to encourage donations and giving from borrowed monies, in view of the ever increasing number of Christians becoming victims of bad debt, (unable to pay their credit cards and loans)? Are we not making the people of God liars and thieves in the eyes of God and the world? Are such acts not weakening our testimony before the unbelieving world and taking us back into the bondage from which we have been redeemed?

Should not the root, stem, and the fruit of the holy vine be alike? Should not the means justify the end? It may be true, and sometimes arguable that, the majority of Christians pay off their credit cards and loans, but what about the many who are unable to pay? Are we not making them bad stewards instead of faithful ones?

"He that loveth his brother abideth in the light, and there is none occasion of stumbling in him (1 John 2:10)

What about vowing? What about the many Christians who are made to vow year after year unable to pay? Are they also not being made to stumble and lie before God? Has the Christian call to life of simplicity, modesty, godly contentment taken a back seat? What about competition among local congregations? A competition, which seems to be growing out of control by each passing day: Churches competing in lofty church buildings, congregation size, best paid ministers, well dressed and good looking ministers, best choir, titles, the most influential speaker, personal aggrandizements and lofty lifestyle:

> "For we must all appear before the judgment seat of Christ; that every one may receive the things done in his body, according to that he hath done, whether it be good or bad, for we must all stand before the judgment seat of Christ" (2 Corinthians 5:10, 12-13).

I believe if individual Christians can spend a little extra time or set aside each day, a little time to thoroughly study the scriptures for themselves and follow the leading of the Holy Spirit, they may save themselves from been exploited by unrighteous and ungodly brethren: "My people are destroyed for lack of knowledge" (Hosea 4:6):

> "I speak to your shame. Is it so, that there is not a wise man among you? No, not one that shall be able to judge between his brethren?" (1 Corinthians 6:5).

Another danger threatening our liberty in Christ are the many forms of worship being introduced into the church; forms that are foreign and alien to the faith. These new ways and forms have become barriers and great hindrances to the move of the Spirit and even to new and genuine seekers. Some churches have introduced what the apostle Paul calls weak and beggarly elements, which in fact are no new truths or better ways, but bondage to the worshippers:

"But now, after that ye have known God, or rather are known of God, how turn ye again to the weak and beggarly elements, whereunto ye desire again to be in bondage? Ye observe days, and months, and times, and years" (Galatians 4:9).

"Of how much sorer punishment, suppose ye, shall he be thought worthy, who hath trodden under foot the Son of God, and hath counted the blood of the covenant, wherewith he was sanctified, an unholy thing, and hath done despite unto the Spirit of grace?" (Mathew 23:23).

My prayer is that the Good Lord would send in more faithful laborers into His vineyard in accordance to His promise: "And I will give you pastors according to mine heart, which shall feed you with knowledge and understanding" (Jeremiah 3:15). I pray that all true and faithful ministers of the Gospel would take a stand to preach, teach and edify the body to accomplish the purpose unto which we are all called:

"Till we all come in the unity of the faith, and of the knowledge of the Son of God, unto a perfect man, unto the measure of the stature of the fulness of Christ: that we henceforth be no more children, tossed to and fro, and carried about with every wind of doctrine, by the sleight of men, and cunning craftiness, whereby they lie in wait to deceive" (Ephesians 4:13-14).

Christians must not follow the disappointing ways of the Old Testament brethren: "Many pastors have destroyed my vineyard, they have trodden my portion under foot, and they have made my pleasant portion a desolate wilderness" (Jeremiah 12:10; cf. 2:8; 3:15; 10:21; 22:22; 23:1-2). We must be aware of the holy name of God (Romans 2:4). We cannot afford to fail the grace of God; we cannot afford to fall short of that which God expects of us as under-shepherds of His church (Hebrews 12:13). We must not allow the ignorant and uninformed to treat the Christian faith or doctrine like any other man-made religion.

It is very important that every Christian know with certainty the bondage from which he has been emancipated and the state of liberty which is now ours in Christ. I believe I can tabulate a few benefits of our liberty in Christ and in the Spirit.

Christians have been freed from:

1. The curse of the Law (Galatians 3:13)
2. Bondage to the law (Galatians 2:19; 4:15)
3. The vain manner of life (1 Peter 1:18)
4. Being slaves to Satan (Acts 26:18)
5. Bondage to the law of sin (Romans 8:2)
6. Death; Wages of sin (Romans 8:2)
7. All unrighteousness (Romans 6:2, 7, 22; 1Peter 2:24)
8. All ungodliness (Isaiah 53:1-11)
9. All iniquity (Titus 2:14)
10. Fear (Romans 8:15; Hebrews 13:6)
11. Guilt (Romans 3:24)
12. The wrath of God (1 Thessalonians 5:9)
13. Darkness (Acts 26:18)
14. The rudiments of the world (Colossians 2:20)
15. The slavish fear of God (Romans 8:15)
16. Over-anxious care (Mathew 6:25-34; 10:29-31)
17. Demons (Romans 8:15)
18. The wrath to come (Luke 3:7)
19. Spiritual bankruptcy (2 Corinthians 8:9)
20. Traditions of men (Colossians 2:8)

In conclusion, Christian liberty is freedom in the Spirit; it is total freedom from sin, the wages of sin and legalism: "Now the Lord is that Spirit: and where the Spirit of the Lord is, there is liberty. Every Christian must stand fast in the liberty wherewith Christ hath made us free, and be not entangled again with the yoke of bondage. We have been called into liberty; however, we must not use our liberty as a license to engage in fleshly lust, but by love serve God and one another.

As God's free people, we cannot use our liberty as a cloke of maliciousness, but as the servants of God. Whosoever looketh into the perfect law of liberty, and continueth therein, he being not a forgetful hearer, but a doer of the work, this man shall be blessed in his deed (cf. James 1:25). "So speak ye, and so do, as they that shall be judged by the law of liberty." Amen.

Notes

Chapter Seven

FRUIT OF THE SPIRIT

 The fruit of the Spirit is the life of Jesus Christ reproduced in and lived through a Christian who is in vital union with Him by the Holy Spirit. The fruit of the Spirit are not products of self effort or characters that a man can produce by self effort. They are fruit of the Spirit and not of the flesh. They are virtues that belong exclusively to God.

Only the Holy Spirit can cause such fruit to show forth in the practical life of the regenerate. The fruit is in singular because it is one fruit bearing nine elements. Our union with Christ produces the spiritual fruit that is expected of us by God. Each of us is given a mandate to be fruitful, to exhibit holy characters, and to do good works through the Spirit's enablement:

> "But the fruit of the Spirit is love, joy, peace, longsuffer-ing, gentleness, goodness, faith, meekness, temperance: against such there is no law" (Galatians 5:22-23).

Christianity is the making of the sons of God; it is the preparation for the revelation of the sons of God on the day of the Lord. A day for which the whole creation is anxiously waiting (Romans 8:19). The stakes are high, but achievable. Every Christian is born in righteousness and true holiness. We are born in Christ with the blue print of holiness:

"Whoever is born of God doth not commit sin; for his seed remaineth in him: and he cannot sin, because he is born of God" (1 John 3:9).

Jesus is the vine; we are the branches. The once-and-for-all redemption by Christ not only makes the sinner a saint but also positions him in Christ (Hebrews 10:10,14). Each of us is grafted into the True Vine (Jesus) by the Holy Spirit. The Spirit is the life of both the vine and the branches. The branches, firmly established, bear more fruit to the glory and joy of God the Father, who is both the owner and gardener:

"I am the true vine, and my Father is the husbandman. Every branch in me that beareth not fruit he taketh away: and every branch that beareth fruit, he purgeth it, that it may bring forth more fruit. Now ye are clean through the word which I have spoken unto you.

Abide in me, and I in you. As the branch cannot bear fruit of itself, except it abide in the vine; no more can ye, except ye abide in me. I am the vine, ye are the branches: He that abideth in me, and I in him, the same bringeth forth much fruit: for without me ye can do nothing.

If a man abide not in me, he is cast forth as a branch, and is withered; and men gather them, and cast them into the fire, and they are burned. If ye abide in me, and my words abide in you, ye shall ask what ye will, and it shall be done unto you. Herein is my Father glorified, that ye bear much fruit; so shall ye be my disciples" (John 15:1-8).

The attention of the gardener is constantly on the vine; His eyes are on the vine. He prunes every branch so that they may bear much fruit. He cuts off non-fruit bearing branches so that those bearing fruits can bear more fruits. But, if a branch does not bear fruit at all, He cuts off that branch because He expects fruit from every branch.

Christians are God's investment; having sowed the life of His Son in us, He expects the holy life of His Son reproduced in and through us, so that the world might see His grace and glory:

> "But now being made free from sin, and become servants to God, ye have your fruit unto holiness, and the end everlasting life" (Romans 6:22)

> "Wherefore, my brethren, ye also are become dead to the law by the body of Christ; that ye should be married to another, even to him who is raised from the dead, that we should bring forth fruit unto God" (Romans 7:4).

> "That ye might walk worthy of the Lord unto all pleasing, being fruitful in every good work, and increasing in the knowledge of God" (Colossians 1:10).

Just as a branch cannot bear fruit on its own unless it abides in the vine, likewise, we cannot do anything without Christ. Without the Spirit, no Christian can do anything worthy of pleasing God. Without the Spirit, we are dead and unfruitful; our own works are considered dead works.

Every branch that is grafted in by the Spirit is correctly positioned; it remains attached to the vine, and therefore, bears fruit. The fruit cannot be different from what is expected. If the vine is good, then the fruit must also be good; if the vine is holy, then the branches and the fruit must also be holy (as He is, so are we). Even though perfection in this life for the regenerate is unattainable in view of our present unredeemed body and the environment, with the indwelling Spirit each of us can live a life without sin; we are able not to sin:

> "For a good tree bringeth not forth corrupt fruit; neither doth a corrupt tree bring forth good fruit. For every tree is known by his own fruit. For of thorns men do not gather figs, nor of a bramble bush gather they grapes" (Luke 6:43-44).

Every branch is fed from the same sap that flows through the whole vine. Grafted branches become one with the vine: Root, stem, branches and fruits belong to each other. Christians are not just followers but disciples - adherents who accept the master's instruction and make it a rule of conduct (Romans 8:23; 1 John 2:2):

"For if the firstfruit be holy, the lump is also holy: and if the root be holy, so are the branches" (Romans 11:16).

Holding on to the faith of Christ would cause us to be fruitful; the power of the Holy Spirit would freely flow through us causing us to bear much more fruit to the pleasure of the Father. The life of Christ will flow freely in and through the life of the Christian:

"Until the spirit be poured upon us from on high, and the wilderness be a fruitful field, and the fruitful field be counted for a forest" (Isaiah 32:15).

Any branch that bears no fruit and as a result cut off from the vine, withers, dry up and dies. This means this branch has lost everything because it did not take advantage of being in the vine to produce good fruit. It missed the purpose for which it was grafted into the vine. In like manner, many Christians may lose their reward at the judgment seat of Christ, even though their souls may be saved:

"If any man's work abide which he hath built thereupon, he shall receive a reward. If any man's work shall be burned, he shall suffer loss: but he himself shall be saved; yet so as by fire" (1 Corinthians 3:14-15).

But, note this, if a branch does not abide in Him (vine), then the branch has never been grafted in the vine by the Spirit. Even though this branch apparently may bear some resemblance to that of a grafted branch, it is false and the fruit is also false.

This false branch as may be called represents a professing Christian. The natural man trying to live like a spiritual man by his own effort is unprofitable. It is a non-Christian working hard to be morally correct or live like one; these could be religious people or what the world might consider good people; people who are upright in their own eyes.

Further, this could be a man who is trying to please God through carnal means; a man who knows all about God, but has never committed his life to Him or born again. Furthermore, this could also be a church-man; a man who attends church regularly and reads the bible daily yet, lives like the devil. He has no Jesus in his heart. This is a man who has religion, but no Christ. "If a man abide not in me, he is cast forth as a branch, and is withered; and men gather them, and cast them into the fire, and they are burned."

> **"Strive to enter in at the strait gate: for many, I say unto you, will seek to enter in, and shall not be able. When once the master of the house is risen up, and hath shut to the door, and ye begin to stand without, and to knock at the door, saying, Lord, Lord, open unto us; and he shall answer and say unto you, I know you not whence ye are:**
>
> **Then shall ye begin to say, We have eaten and drunk in thy presence, and thou hast taught in our streets. But he shall say, I tell you, I know you not whence ye are; depart from me, all ye workers of iniquity"** (Luke 13:24-27).

Although a professing Christian may outwardly appear morally apt in the sight of men, He is not better or holier than a non-Christian (unbeliever). Both are considered trees standing on their own and ready to be hewn down and cast into the fire:

> **"And now also the axe is laid unto the root of the trees: every tree therefore which bringeth not forth good fruit is hewn down, and cast into the fire"** (Luke 3:9).

> **"Every tree that bringeth not forth good fruit is hewn down, and cast into the fire"** (Mathew 7:19).

The fearful, the unbelieving, the abominable, the murderers, the whoremongers, the sorcerers, the idolaters, and all liars (including professing Christians), shall have their part in the lake which burns with fire and brimstone: which is the second death (Revelations 21:8); all those who have their names in the books but, not in the book of life, shall appear before the great white throne of God (Revelations 20:11-12). Because they refused the mercy and the grace of God through Jesus Christ, their names were not written in the Lamb's book of life (Philippians 4:3; Revelations 3:5; 13:8; 17:8). Non-Christians are on their own; they are without Christ and would therefore, be judged according to their own works.

The life of a Christian from start to finish is all about the Spirit of God: Spirit-called, Spirit-born, Spirit-indwelt, and Spirit-led, Spirit fruit-bearing and Spirit-gifted. If these things be, we shall be changed from glory to glory by the Spirit into the exact image of Christ daily. I pray the Lord to grant us grace to understand this mysterious and powerful life that is set before us in Christ. We are born again to produce fruit of righteousness (good works).

Every tree is known by its fruit. Before we became born again, we bore certain kind of fruits. We were by nature children of the devil, and produced fruits that were in conformity to his nature. We cursed, lied, cheated, and our minds were filled with dead works. This was our normal way of life; it was absolutely impossible for us not to sin. We were ignorant of God's ways and righteousness (Romans 6:21). But, praise be to God, we are now servants of God; we are servants of righteousness and partakers of the divine nature.

We are now branches of the true vine; the old tree is no more. Now, we bear righteous fruits - fruits that are worthy of our new nature and well pleasing to God. Grafted into Christ, it is no longer we that liveth, but Christ who lives in us: "For to me to live is Christ, and to die is gain" (Philippians 1:21). We are held by the vine and sustained by its roots. In Christ, we are as secured in God as Christ is in God. We shall never perish and neither can any creature pluck us out of the hands of the living God (John 11:28).

Death for a Christian is a blessing; it is a great gain (absent from this world, we are at home with the Lord): "Precious in the sight of the Lord is the death of His saints (Psalm 116:15). From the moment of salvation the Holy Spirit keeps working in and through us daily until Christ is formed in us; until we are filled with the fruits of righteousness; until we produce the fruit of the Spirit and abound unto every good work:

> **"Being filled with the fruits of righteousness, which are by Jesus Christ, unto the glory and praise of God"** (Philippians 1:11).

God is greatly praised when His children bear much fruit. We are truly the light of the world when we live clean before God and man, then the name of the Lord is magnified among men. When Christians walk right, darkness (ignorance) is dispelled and perishing souls are saved. Likewise, if we fail, His name is blasphemed among men.

As the salt of this world, we can, by our righteous deeds, delay and probably stop the worms of sin from destroying the souls of men who are created in the image and likeness of God. When Christians are full of salt, wounded souls become healed and cold stony hearts receive hearts of flesh:

> **"Let your light so shine before men, that they may see your good works, and glorify your Father which is in heaven"** (Mathew 5:16).

> **"Having your conversation honest among the Gentiles: that, whereas they speak against you as evildoers, they may by your good works, which they shall behold, glorify God in the day of visitation"** (1 Peter 2:12).

As new members of God's household, we are not only expected to put off the old man, but also put on the new man that resembles God in holiness and righteousness. New life and good fruit are for new men; there is no room for any other life or fruit:

> "Bring forth therefore fruits meet for repentance" (Mathew 3:6).

"Be ye holy for I am holy" (1 Peter 1:16), is a common denominator of all Christians; it covers the whole spectrum of transcended life:

> "How God anointed Jesus of Nazareth with the Holy Ghost and with power: who went about doing good, and healing all that were oppressed of the devil; for God was with him" (Acts 10:38).

> "Pure religion and undefiled before God and the Father is this, To visit the fatherless and widows in their affliction, and to keep himself unspotted from the world" (James 1:27).

> "Charge them that are rich in this world, that they be not highminded, nor trust in uncertain riches, but in the living God, who giveth us richly all things to enjoy; that they do good, that they be rich in good works, ready to distribute, willing to communicate; laying up in store for themselves a good foundation against the time to come, that they may lay hold on eternal life" (1 Timothy 6:17-19.

Summary of the fruits:

"But the fruit of the Spirit is love, joy, peace, longsuffering, gentleness, goodness, faith, meekness, temperance: against such there is no law."

1. Love: Listed first because it is the foundation of all other graces. God is love and loved the world so much that He gave His only begotten Son as a sin offering. The self-denying, self-sacrificing love of Christ is that which Spirit-led Christians manifest (John 3:16; 1 John 4:8).

2. Joy: The joy of the Lord is the believer's strength. This joy is independent of external circumstances; it an inner spring from peace and union with Christ by the Holy Spirit (1 Thessalonians 1:6).

3. Peace: Tranquility of soul (Philippians 4:4-7). Again this is peace from God and not as a result of external conditions: "Peace I leave with you, my peace I give unto you: not as the world giveth, give I unto you. Let not your heart be troubled, neither let it be afraid" (John 14:27). It is an inner repose and tranquility, even in the face of persecutions and trials.

4. Longsuffering: Patient endurance and steadfastness under provocation (2 Corinthians 6:6; Colossians 1:11; 3:12). It entertains no thought and desire of revenge or retaliation even when wronged.

5. Gentleness: kindness, kindly disposition and graciousness disposition. The best example is that which God has demonstrated towards sinners (Romans 2:4; Ephesians 2:7).

6. Goodness: Beneficence, ready to do good; it is love in action. Springs of good deeds issuing from a heart full of compassion and righteousness.

7. Faith: Faithfulness, fidelity; that quality that renders a person reliable or trustworthy. That which makes one true to his promise and faithful to his task (e.g. Luke 16:10-12).

8. Meekness: Not weakness, but controlled strength. Submissive to every word that comes from the mouth of the Lord; a listening ear (James 1:21). Unselfishness

to fellow man; treat others in the way you would like to be treated.

9. Temperance: Self-control, rational restraint of the natural impulses; denotes self-mastery.

Against the fruit of the Spirit, there is no law; holy character and the law are embedded in the Christian. Holy traits are products of the Holy Spirit which only the born again can exhibit. Again, the common denominator of all Christians is holiness in life and service to God and man, for we cannot afford to be "like the dog that turns to his own vomit again; and the sow that returns to the mire" (2 Peter 2:22).

In conclusion, the fruit of righteousness, which is by Christ Jesus, is all that God expects of every Christian. This fruit cannot be produced by human power or self, but only by the Holy Spirit. Born of the Spirit, each individual Christian already possesses the fruit, and daily, each of us increasingly becomes aware and reckons it to be so in practical living - in life and service. This is a duty of Christians.

The world would be a better place if Christians could only allow the Holy Spirit to live the life of Christ in and through them. Also, the mouth of many critics would be silenced; God's name would be highly praised and joy would be brought to us as well. The earth would be filled with the glory of God. Holy characters are the product of the divine nature. Christians are new men with divine characters.

Chapter Eight

GIFTS OF THE SPIRIT

 Every Christian is gifted. As spiritual beings, we possess a Spiritual gift or gifts. These are gifts of power or supernatural gifts, which are given to each by the Holy Spirit. They are gifts of grace, and are not meritorious. You cannot work for them and neither can they be earned.

They are priceless and absolutely free for all; they are free for every Christian because Jesus has already paid for them. By His own will, the Spirit releases them for the work of the ministry and for the profit of all. Every Christian is blessed with Spiritual gifts:

"But unto every one of us is given grace according to the measure of the gift of Christ" (Ephesians 4:7).

God has: "Blessed us with all spiritual blessings in the heavenly places in Christ Jesus" (Ephesians 1:3), and among these blessings and freely given to us are Spiritual gifts; the gifts of the Spirit. Indwelt by the Spirit, Christians possess Spiritual gifts; we have the potential to demonstrate the particular gift that has been given to the praise and glory of our Lord.

Just as we need talents and gifts for natural existence, so we need spiritual gifts for spiritual existence. Every Christian has his proper gift of God, one after this manner and another after that:

"As every man hath received the gift, even so minister the same one to another, as good stewards of the manifold grace of God" (1 Peter 4:10).

The purpose of these gifts is for individual and collective establishment. They are given for the profit of every man in the body of Christ:

"But the manifestation of the Spirit is given to every man to profit withal" (1 Corinthians 12:7).

It is extremely important that each individual Christian know that he is gifted by God. We begin the Christian life already loaded with gifts. Knowing that you have them and allowing them to manifest, makes us a blessing one to another. We must, therefore, be aware and not wallow in ignorance. Such knowledge is important, because it enhances personal prayer life and produces great results in witnessing for Christ:

"Now concerning spiritual gifts, brethren, I would not have you ignorant" (1 Corinthians 12:1).

The beauty and greatness of transcended life is that every Christian has some gifts for the benefit of all. We brought nothing to the table for our salvation, but we have so much to bring to the table from salvation. As the coming of our Lord and Savior Jesus Christ tarries, these gifts are given to all believers just to do that - to continue the work of evangelism till He comes:

"So that ye come behind in no gift; waiting for the coming of our Lord Jesus Christ" (1 Corinthians 1:7).

Spiritual gifts, often called charismatic gifts by some, rightfully belong to the Holy Spirit. Both the fruit (holy characters) and the gifts are His. The Spirit gives to each of us at the moment of salvation, but the time of usage or manifestation differs with each individual Christian. Some Christians identify their gifts early or soon after salvation, others later and some never. Operating in the gifts may depend on exposure and acceptance of the truth as set forth in scripture.

Spiritual gifts are not natural talents or natural endowments. The qualifying term, "Spiritual," differentiates them from the natural. It is "Spiritual," in the sense that, it comes directly from the Holy Spirit, and not through the process of natural birth and selective education. That which is born natural, is natural and that which is born of the Spirit is spirit. Spiritual gifts are for the Spirit born.

Even though some of the Spirit's manifestations assume the nature of the secular or natural, they are always achieved without prior training or experience. They are neither the raising of natural endowments to a higher level and neither is it the work of witchcraft or magic. These gifts are supernatural and only manifest when the Spirit takes possession of the believer and uses the members of his body; that is, mouth, hands and body for the service of Christ.

Let me give you an example to clarify the just stated point. An outsider may frown at the mention that God was the builder of the tabernacle (the ark of covenant) because natural talents, especially that of a skilled artisan, carpenter or craftsman may easily produce such a product. It may not even require spiritual gifts if man is building the same for himself.

But, this is God's project and must be done strictly according to His specification, under His direction, and with gifted endowments and not from natural talents or acquired knowledge. God was the source, and the means; the outcome was for His own glory, yet the whole project assumed the appearance of the natural work:

"And the LORD spake unto Moses, saying, see, I have called by name Bezaleel the son of Uri, the son of Hur, of the tribe of Judah: And I have filled him with the spirit

of God, in wisdom, and in understanding, and in knowledge, and in all manner of workmanship, to devise cunning works, to work in gold, and in silver, and in brass, and in cutting of stones, to set them, and in carving of timber, to work in all manner of workmanship.

And I, behold, I have given with him Aholiab, the son of Ahisamach, of the tribe of Dan: and in the hearts of all that are wise hearted I have put wisdom, that they may make all that I have commanded thee; the tabernacle of the congregation, and the ark of the testimony, and the mercy seat that is thereupon, and all the furniture of the tabernacle, and the table and his furniture, and the pure candlestick with all his furniture, and the altar of incense,

And the altar of burnt offering with all his furniture, and the laver and his foot, And the cloths of service, and the holy garments for Aaron the priest, and the garments of his sons, to minister in the priest's office. And the anointing oil, and sweet incense for the holy place: according to all that I have commanded thee shall they do" (Exodus 31:1-11).

To determine what constitutes the work of God, the source, the means, and the end result must be of God and for His glory; the Spirit must be the source that provides the strength and wisdom without human experience. For example, God can use a Christian who has no knowledge of playing the piano, to play or produce the most skillful performance on piano.

Nothing is impossible with God. Of course, there may be human involvement in all works of God, but that does not rob it from being the work only God can do. There is always a unity of source and purpose in the work of the Spirit. The purpose of all supernatural works without exception is for the glory of God.

Now, here is a little definition; spiritual gifts are concrete manifestations of the grace of God; they are special energy (ability, power,) bestowed upon each and every Christians for use in the service of Christ and for the benefit of all believers (the church). Do not think it strange that God would give to each of His children gifts by His spirit, for He that spared not his own Son, but delivered him up for us all, shall not hesitate also with him to freely give us all things (Romans 8:32).

There are several gifts for the body of Christ. There are diversities of gifts, for different services to the Lord Jesus Christ, by the same heavenly Father who is the source of all the gifts, and the same Holy Spirit who dispenses them to each of us according to His own will for the profit of all believers.

> **"Now there are diversities of gifts, but the same Spirit. And there are differences of administrations, but the same Lord. And there are diversities of operations, but it is the same God which worketh all in all. But the manifestation of the Spirit is given to every man to profit withal"** (1 Corinthians 12:1-7).

As already mentioned, the gifts are diverse and many, except the Lord, no man knows how many there are, and since no man knows how many, it must also follow that no Christian has them all:

> **"For as we have many members in one body, and all members have not the same office: So we, being many, are one body in Christ, and every one members one of another"** (Romans 12:4-5).

Paul graciously listed a few of the gifts and also gave us insight on some of them:

> **"For to one is given by the Spirit the word of wisdom; to another the word of knowledge by the same Spirit; to another faith by the same Spirit; to another the gifts of healing by the same Spirit; to another the working of miracles; to another prophecy; to another discerning of spirits; to another divers kinds of tongues; to another the interpretation of tongues:**

But all these worketh that one and the selfsame Spirit, dividing to every man severally as he will" (1 Corinthians 12:8-11).

"Having then gifts differing according to the grace that is given to us, whether prophecy, let us prophesy according to the proportion of faith; or ministry, let us wait on our ministering: or he that teacheth, on teaching;

or he that exhorteth, on exhortation: he that giveth, let him do it with simplicity; he that ruleth, with diligence; he that sheweth mercy, with cheerfulness" (Romans 12:6-8).

Not only has the Spirit of Christ given to each member of His body a spiritual gift (gifts) in addition, the Spirit has given certain gifted Christians as gifts to the church. These are men chosen for special work in the body. These men are not the product of any institution, local church, or personal preference. God employs His own workers; He alone chooses His workers and assigns to each their responsibilities within and outside His body. The Spirit selects these men for the service of Christ. The ministry of these chosen men may be what some call, the five-fold ministry:

"It was he who gave some to be apostles, some to be prophets, some to be evangelists, and some to be pastors and teachers" (Ephesians 4:11).

Now, you can appreciate how pastors, evangelists, etc., are called or chosen and that one cannot make or appoint himself a member of the five-fold. The Spirit first gives gifts to every Christian, then selects some gifted Christians for special services for the establishment of the whole church. The purpose for this second phase of the gifts, that is the gift of gifted men are:

"For the perfecting of the saints, for the work of the ministry, for the edifying of the body of Christ: Till we all come in the unity of the faith, and of the knowledge of the Son of God, unto a perfect man, unto the measure of the stature of the fulness of Christ:

That we henceforth be no more children, tossed to and fro, and carried about with every wind of doctrine, by the sleight of men, and cunning craftiness, whereby they lie in wait to deceive; but speaking the truth in love, may grow up into Him in all things, which is the head, even Christ" (Ephesians 4:12-14).

Apostles, prophets, evangelists, pastors and teachers are special gifts for the entire body of Christ and may not be for any private group, denomination or non-denominational church (or congregation). The choice of gifted men is the prerogative of the divine; God chooses, ordains, and assigns responsibility to each as He wills; they are directly under His supervision.

God can assign any of them to wherever His sheep may be found - any time, any place, and any where. They move by His impulse and not by denominational demands. None are chosen or called by men, and none are by his own authority. Jesus is the chief shepherd, and those He chooses for His work are under-shepherds:

"And when the chief Shepherd shall appear, ye shall receive a crown of glory that fadeth not away" (1 Peter 5:4).

Apostles are sent as authoritative delegates. For Christians who believe they are called to be apostles, here are the signs. It may help with the knowledge of recognizing an apostle as:

"Truly the signs of an apostle were wrought among you in all patience, in signs, and wonders, and mighty deeds" (2 Corinthians 12:12).

Prophets in the New Testament seem to have additional functions compared to their Old Testament counter-parts. In addition to being foretellers and forth-tellers they provide edification, exhortation, and comfort (1Corinthians 14:3). Evangelists are those who spread the Gospel from place to place; itinerant preachers and missionaries fall into this group.

Pastors and teachers are listed together, maybe for the reason that they belong to one office; one office with two functions. Practically, pastors always do both; they shepherd the congregation as well as instruct them in God's ways (cf. John 21:16; Acts 20:8; 1 Peter 5:2). Their duty includes shepherding, mobilizing and training the saints.

Further, in addition to these, the church sometimes appoints elders or overseers who teach and look after the flock (Acts 20:28; 1 Peter 2:25; 5:4). An elder denotes the dignity of the office and an overseer or bishop denotes duties. The qualifications for these offices are clearly stated in the scriptures (cf. 1 Timothy 3:2ff; Titus 1:9ff).

All these callings are purely by grace. God does not choose leaders based on personal merits, favoritism, charisma, education, family affiliation and social standing:

"For there is no respect of persons with God" (Romans 2:11).

There is a popular belief among some Christians that, Spiritual gifts, especially those of power, are no longer in operation or needed. This is far from the truth. Both gifts - Spiritual and gifted men will never cease as long as the work of the ministry continues. The ministry of soul winning and the training of the saints shall continue until our Lord returns.

Believe it or not, God will also continue to confirm His word using signs, wonders and miracles as the Gospel of Christ is preached. Jesus, who went about doing good and healing all those who were sick and oppressed, as long as He tarries, will continue to do the work He has begun by His Spirit through His faithful and believing disciples:

"God also bearing them witness, both with signs and wonders, and with divers miracles, and gifts of the Holy Ghost, according to his own will?" (Hebrews 2:4).

Further, God who wishes the good of all has not changed; He remains the compassionate, caring, forgiving, and kind God who is not willing to see any man perish. He still cares for this generation just as He did in the generation of the apostles.

It is true that when Jesus comes, gifts and the gift of men will cease, but until then, let us continue the good work for which purpose these supernatural gifts are given. Let each of us through the signs, wonders, miracles, and gifts of the Spirit do the work of God. Let us continue to heal the sick, raise the dead, and cast out demons until the day of His arrival (cf. Revelations 11): "And he passed in front of Moses, proclaiming, "The LORD, the LORD, the compassionate and gracious God, slow to anger, abounding in love and faithfulness" (Exodus 34:6).

The good works of preaching and praying for the unsaved, helping the poor, healing the sick, casting out devils to relieve the oppressed and possessed and such like can only be accomplished through supernatural gifts: "For we are his workmanship, created in Christ Jesus unto good works, which God hath before ordained that we should walk in them" (Ephesians 2:10).

It is for His glory to demonstrate to all creatures how good and kind God is through the power gifts. Jesus Christ definitely left us examples to follow:

"How God anointed Jesus of Nazareth with the Holy Ghost and with power: who went about doing good, and healing all that were oppressed of the devil; for God was with him" (Acts 10:38).

Again, for our dear saints who believe that the gifts ceased with the death of the apostles of Christ. I have this to say: The gifts were not meant for the apostles, but for His church. As long as Jesus remains on the throne, and the church remains on earth, the work of the ministry would not cease.

Further, as long as the Holy Spirit remains with the individual saints and with His church, the gifts would not cease. Furthermore, as long as Satan is among us, and also the sick, weak, possessed, and the lost, the witness of the Spirit would not cease. Amen. Besides, spiritual gifts are in two groups as already mentioned: Spiritual gifts and gifted men. Since both gifts have the same source and purpose if one group ceases, the other must also cease.

For example, if the gifts of signs, miracles, healings, and tongue and interpretation cease, then apostles, prophets, teachers, pastors and teachers must also cease. Man made titles like Archbishops, Most reverend, chief shepherd, presiding bishop, etc., have all ceased. Then, let us stop calling men pastors, bishops and so forth because they have all ceased.

We cannot pick and choose which part of God's word to believe and not to believe. The bible is not subject to any man's private interpretation (2 Peter 1:20). If we choose to believe, then let us believe all: "All scripture is given by inspiration of God, and is profitable for doctrine, for reproof, for correction, for instruction in righteousness: That the man of God may be perfect, thoroughly furnished unto all good works" (2 Timothy 3:16-17). Equally, if we choose not to belief some, then let us deny all.

But, praise is to the Lord, since the Lord of the church is still endowing men with the spiritual gifts and calling some into his vineyard as co-laborers, let us pray to Him to empower us. There are untold needs and sufferings in the church and in the world and the only way the church can help alleviate some of these is through the gifts:

"Therefore said he unto them. The harvest truly is great, but the labourers are few: pray ye therefore the Lord of the harvest, that he would send forth labourers into his harvest" (Luke 10:2).

The glory and the beauty of these gifts is hard to measure. Their effect on those who choose to believe, users, beneficiaries, and witnesses alike are immeasurable. These gifts produce joy unprecedented; not only do they attract huge crowds who come to listen to the Gospel preached but they also produce rapturous praise, thanksgiving, and glory to God from the lips of all witnesses. They solidify individual faith. Also, the kingdom of Christ grows exponentially as the Lord adds to the church them who ought to be saved (Acts 2:47):

> "Those who accepted his message were baptized, and about three thousand were added to their number that day" (Acts 2:41).

> "And immediately he arose, took up the bed, and went forth before them all; insomuch that they were all amazed, and glorified God, saying, We never saw it on this fashion" (Mark 2:12; cf. Acts 3:8).

> "And by the hands of the apostles were many signs and wonders wrought among the people; (and they were all with one accord in Solomon's porch. And of the rest durst no man join himself to them: but the people magnified them. And believers were the more added to the Lord, multitudes both of men and women" (Acts 5:12-14).

> "Ye also helping together by prayer for us, that for the gift bestowed upon us by the means of many persons thanks may be given by many on our behalf" (2 Corinthians 1:11).

The only qualification or pre-condition to receiving these gifts is to be born again; born and indwelt by the Spirit. As already mentioned, it is free for every regenerate:

> "Then Peter said unto them, Repent, and be baptized every one of you in the name of Jesus Christ for the re-mission of sins, and ye shall receive the gift of the Holy Ghost" (Acts 2:38).

Like our salvation, these gifts are irrevocable. Once given, it is forever given. If you have it, you have it forever. Forever means till we go home to glory or He comes for us. He is not a flip flop

God. Being under His grace and mercy, there is no limit as to how far each of us can grow in Him or how much He can use us individually and collectively to accomplish His purpose. His grace is shoreless, bottomless, and immeasurable. Remember, we did not ask for the Spirit and neither did we qualify to host Him, but God, who is willing to show how kind and merciful He is, freely gave Him to us. Likewise, we don't qualify for the gifts but, He gives them freely to us all:

"For the gifts and calling of God are without repentance" (Romans 11:29):

Further, does the omniscient not know all that each of us Christians will ever do before He chose us? Did He not know what we were capable of before He gave us birth again? (cf. Psalm 139). My advice to every believer is to enjoy the gifts of the Spirit while they are available.

Only you can stop yourself, either by quitting from using them or from asking for them. How far in God, is up to each of us to decide. You do well if you obey, for the day of reward is very close; the day for the prize of our good works draws near.

Further still, the Holy Spirit loves each of us dearly; He would not hesitate to grant our request for the gifts if we are occupied with the kingdom business and if our heart is full of compassion:

"Pure religion and undefiled before God and the Father is this, to visit the fatherless and widows in their affliction, and to keep himself unspotted from the world" (James 1:27).

Gifted Christians can be used by the Spirit as instruments to gift other Christians or manifest any embedded gifts; especially, through prayer and the laying of hands. Even though every Christian is gifted as co-laborers with God, we have His promise to ask for other gifts that may be needed for the work of the ministry:

"And this is the confidence that we have in him that, if we ask any thing according to his will, he heareth us" (1 John 5:14).

"Then laid they their hands on them, and they received the Holy Ghost" (Acts 8:17; 6:6).

"And when Paul had laid his hands upon them, the Holy Ghost came on them; and they spake with tongues, and prophesied" (Acts 19:6).

For example, Paul in his letter to the church in Rome expressed how he longed to be with them that he may impart unto them some spiritual gifts (Romans 1:11). As long as we watch and pray and allow the Spirit to rule our new life, we are bound to bear fruit unto His praise and glory. When our life, filled with fruit and gifts for service are in sync with His will, the Spirit will use us in such a way as to bring glory to our Lord; He will teach us what to say and what to do:

"Now go; I will help you speak and will teach you what to say. You shall speak to him and put words in his mouth; I will help both of you speak and will teach you what to do" (Exodus 4:12,15).

We will decree a thing and it shall come to pass (Job 22:28). For example, the prophet Elijah would say: "As the LORD God of Israel liveth, before whom I stand, there shall not be dew nor rain these years, but according to my word" (1Kings 17:1), and truly for almost three and half years there was no rain. As co-laborers with God (1Corinthians 3:9), we have His promise that our prayers and requests will be answered if we live and ask according to His will:

"If ye then, being evil, know how to give good gifts unto your children: how much more shall your heavenly Father give the Holy Spirit to them that ask him?" (Luke 11:13).

Jesus is a clear example of what happens to those who obey and have pleasure in doing the will of God. In His ministry, the blind saw, the lamed walked, the dead were raised, diseases were healed, lepers were cleansed, dumb spoke, deaf heard, and demons were cast out. He was full of the Spirit and power.

No doctor or physician can emulate or heal people in the way the gifts of the Spirit do, or in the manner of the Holy Spirit. Men in the days of Jesus wondered not only at His miracle works, but also the gracious words proceeding from His mouth. They were amazed how Jesus could be that brilliant without formal education (John 7:15).

Through the ages, the disciples of Jesus Christ have also demonstrated many times the miracle works of the Spirit, which has always baffled many. For example, when the Jewish leaders: "Saw the boldness of Peter and John, and perceived that they were not learned and ignorant men, they marveled; and acknowledged them, that they had been with Jesus" (Acts 4:13).

As mentioned, Spiritual gifts are as diverse as the human body (1 Corinthians 12:12ff). The Church is a unity in diversity; there is one body but many members:

"For as the body is one, and hath many members, and all the members of that one body, being many, are one body: so also is Christ" (1 Corinthians 12:12; cf. Romans 12:4-5).

"There is one body, and one Spirit, even as ye are called in one hope of your calling; One Lord, one faith, one baptism, One God and Father of all, who is above all, and through all, and in you all" (Ephesians 4:4-6).

This diversity, coupled with the complex nature of the gifts themselves, makes them seemingly difficult to regulate or control; hence, there is a need for sound and open doctrine on the gifts. The present attempt by some church leaders to push them under the carpet is not wise.

Teaching on the gifts is very much needed today as it was in the days of the apostles. It is proper that the Christians be educated in the things of the Spirit to avoid the repeated mistakes that have plagued the church for centuries.

Very often, what we see in the church as the gift of the Spirit in manifestation is nothing but pure confusion, purposelessness, and uncontrolled behavior of ignorant Christians. Ecstasy is no excuse for lack of self-control: "the spirits of the prophets are subject to the prophets" (1 Corinthians 14:32).

Further, Christians for the past centuries have been extricated, ex-communicated, and abused in many ways in both denominational and non-denominational assemblies because of supernatural gifts. These gifts have also contributed largely to the unnecessary break-away and the establishments of local churches with strange doctrines.

If this ignorance among believers is allowed to continue it will only breed more confusion:

> **"For I say, through the grace given unto me, to every man that is among you, not to think of himself more highly than he ought to think; but to think soberly, according as God hath dealt to every man the measure of faith. For as we have many members in one body, and all members have not the same office:**

> **So we, being many, are one body in Christ, and every one members one of another. Having then gifts differing according to the grace that is given to us, whether prophecy, let us prophesy according to the proportion of faith; or ministry, let us wait on our ministering: or he that teacheth, on teaching; or he that exhorteth, on exhortation: he that giveth, let him do it with simplicity; he that ruleth, with diligence; he that sheweth mercy, with"** (Romans 12:3-8).

If we believe that the gifts are for the service of God, then the church must make priority of its teachings. We must not forget the great admonishment: "Let all things be done decently and in order (1 Corinthians 14:26,40; cf. Romans 12:3-8).

Again, how would believers use the gifts in the way of the Spirit, if they are not taught? What would be the role of the five-fold ministry?

"Each one should use whatever gift he has received to serve others, faithfully administering God's grace in its various forms. If anyone speaks, he should do it as one speaking the very words of God. If anyone serves, he should do it with the strength God provides, so that in all things God may be praised through Jesus Christ. To him be the glory and the power for ever and ever. Amen" (1 Peter 4:10-11).

Fruit and gifts of the Spirit go hand in hand in the life and service of every Christian; they compliment each other. The fruit of the Spirit is the bedrock of gifts of the Spirit; the same Holy Spirit provides the believer with both. A Christian who is living the new life in the power of His Spirit is more enduring, of quality and of a sweet-smelling savor to God. A Christian who has the gift of prophecy, but addicted to gossip is likely to fall under repute. Even if such prophecy as uttered has its source in God, it is hard for those who know the moral shortcomings of such to accept the words as divinely inspired:

"As it is written: God's name is blasphemed among the Gentiles because of you" (Romans 2:24).

Even the unbelieving world cherishes a Christian whose life is stainless and full of power. We must possess implacable character, if we truly desire to be used of God and desire to bring glory and honor to His Holy name. Then, the church must follow the examples of her leaders:

"And in those days, when the number of the disciples was multiplied, there arose a murmuring of the Grecians against the Hebrews, because their widows were neglected in the daily ministration.

Then the twelve called the multitude of the disciples unto them, and said, It is not reason that we should leave the word of God, and serve tables.

Wherefore, brethren, look ye out among you seven men of honest report, full of the Holy Ghost and wisdom, whom we may appoint over this business.

But we will give ourselves continually to prayer, and to the ministry of the word.

And the saying pleased the whole multitude: and they chose Stephen, a man full of faith and of the Holy Ghost, and Philip, and Prochorus, and Nicanor, and Timon, and Parmenas, and Nicolas a proselyte of Antioch:

Whom they set before the apostles: and when they had prayed, they laid their hands on them.

And the word of God increased; and the number of the disciples multiplied in Jerusalem greatly; and a great company of the priests were obedient to the faith.

And Stephen, full of faith and power, did great wonders and miracles among the people" (Acts 6:1-8).

Supernaturally born, Christians cannot depend on carnal talents and gifts to do the work of God. Further, since our foes are spiritual beings and not of the flesh, earthly war machines or conventional weapons are useless against them, therefore spiritual weapons are needed. Mortal battles must be fought with mortal weapons and likewise, immortals battles with immortals weapons.

Despite the fact that Christian's live in the same old mortal body, the weapons of our warfare are not carnal:

"For the weapons of our warfare are not carnal, but mighty through God to the pulling down of strongholds;

casting down imaginations, and every high thing that exalted itself against the knowledge of God, and bringing into captivity every thought to the obedience of Christ" (2 Corinthians 10:4-5).

As spiritual beings, we speak spiritual truths. We live and move in the power of the Holy Spirit:

"This is what we speak, not in words taught us by human wisdom but in words taught by the Spirit, expressing spiritual truths in spiritual words. The man without the Spirit does not accept the things that come from the Spirit of God, for they are foolishness to him, and he cannot understand them, because they are spiritually discerned" (1 Corinthians 2:13-14).

The daily life of a Christian should be full of miracles. Walking with God is fun, but full of surprises: "For my thoughts are not your thoughts, neither are your ways my ways, saith the LORD" (Isaiah 55:8). Even though, the Lord has redeemed and called us alongside to work together with Him, He does not rely on the arms of flesh or man and neither does He want us to.

God does not rely on the experience and strength of men to fulfill His mission or accomplish His purpose: "the LORD saveth not with sword and spear" (1 Samuel 17:47):

"Then he answered and spake unto me, saying, This is the word of the LORD unto Zerubbabel, saying, Not by might, nor by power, but by my spirit, saith the LORD of hosts" (Zechariah 4:6).

The same power that was available to the early disciples is available through the gifts of the Spirit to each of us, even now. To all who believe, He gave them power not only to become, but also to live as sons of God. I say to all who love to see the glory of God fill the earth and His name highly exalted; to everyone who needs power to witness or evangelize, fruit and the gifts is the way.

Indwelling Spirit makes weak people strong and the fearful fearless:

"For God hath not given us the spirit of fear; but of power, and of love, and of a sound mind" (2 Timothy 1:7; cf. Proverbs 21:8).

While Jesus was on earth, He gave power to His disciples to do the work of evangelism. Many times, He sent them ahead of Him to preach the good news of the kingdom and not once did He send them without power and authority over all devils, and to cure diseases:

"He said to them, "Go into all the world and preach the good news to all creation. Whoever believes and is baptized will be saved, but whoever does not believe will be condemned.

And these signs will accompany those who believe: In my name they will drive out demons; they will speak in new tongues; they will pick up snakes with their hands; and when they drink deadly poison, it will not hurt them at all; they will place their hands on sick people, and they will get well" (Mark 16:15-18).

"Through mighty signs and wonders, by the power of the Spirit of God; so that from Jerusalem, and round about unto Illyricum, I have fully preached the gospel of Christ" (Romans 15:19; cf. Acts 19:11-12).

Preaching the good news of the kingdom is another form of spiritual warfare; preachers must therefore be armed by the Spirit. As the Gospel is preached, prisoners of Satan are released by the power of God and translated into the Kingdom of Christ and of God: "Go your ways: behold, I send you forth as lambs among wolves" (Luke 10: 3; cf. verse 8).

Christian's need all the power that they can get from the Spirit; I mean all the supernatural gifts available to convince and confront a generation of unbelievers like our generation. The same Jesus, who sent the apostles, sends each individual Christian or believer to do the same work today. Therefore, there is no reason why the Lord would not equip us just as He did in the past:

> **"Then he called his twelve disciples together, and gave them power and authority over all devils, and to cure diseases. And he sent them to preach the kingdom of God, and to heal the sick"** (Luke 9:1-2).

> **"Behold, I give unto you power to tread on serpents and scorpions, and over all the power of the enemy: and nothing shall by any means hurt you"** (Luke 10:19).

The daily life of a believer is a war against strategies and tricks of the devil: "For we wrestle not against flesh and blood, but against principalities, against powers, against the rulers of the darkness of this world, against spiritual wickedness in high places" (Ephesians 6:12). Transcended life is living holy in an unholy world.

Since every Christian has a gift, or is gifted, it is not expected that there should be any jealousy among believers concerning them. After all, it is not who got what, but what is done with that which is given and gotten. We do not all have the same gift (s); the Holy Spirit freely gives certain gifts to certain people according to His own will.

The Spirit who made us knows what is best for each of us and so gives that which He sees fit and needed in accordance to His eternal purpose. Even praying for the gifts must be by His will and revelation.

God would not give to any of us that which we cannot bear or need; every man has his proper gift of God:

> **"But all these worketh that one and the selfsame Spirit, dividing to every man severally as he will"** (1 Corinthians 12:11).

"For I would that all men were even as I myself. But every man hath his proper gift of God, one after this manner, and another after that" (1 Corinthians 7:7).

Likewise, to each of us is given the measure of faith according to the grace of God. We must, therefore, be content with whatever gift that we may possess and use it to the best of our ability, faith, and knowledge and for the good of all:

"Having then gifts differing according to the grace that is given to us, whether prophecy, let us prophesy according to the proportion of faith" (Romans 12:6).

Spiritual gifts are not for personal power, pontification, and enrichment. We must not try to extend ourselves beyond that which is enabled, and always remember that the glory is not ours, but the Lord's. Boasting and arrogance and all such like, must not be allowed to grow in the body of Christ.

To compare ourselves with one another is not wise. If we want to compare and boast, then Christ is the only perfect role model to be compared and in Him we should have our boast: "Shall the axe boast itself against him that heweth therewith? Or shall the saw magnify itself against him that shaketh it? as if the rod should shake itself against them that lift it up, or as if the staff should lift up itself, as if it were no wood" (Isaiah 10:15):

"If any man speak, let him speak as the oracles of God; if any man minister, let him do it as of the ability which God giveth: that God in all things may be glorified through Jesus Christ, to whom be praise and dominion for ever and ever. Amen" (1 Peter 4:10).

"For we dare not make ourselves of the number, or compare ourselves with some that commend themselves: but they measuring themselves by themselves, and comparing themselves among themselves, are not wise.

But we will not boast of things without our measure, but
according to the measure of the rule which God hath dis-
tributed to us, a measure to reach even unto you. For we
stretch not ourselves beyond our measure, as though we
reached not unto you: for we are come as far as to you
also in preaching the gospel of Christ:

Not boasting of things without our measure, that is, of
other men's labours; but having hope, when your faith is
increased, that we shall be enlarged by you according to
our rule abundantly" (2 Corinthians 10:12-15).

The only person worthy of all the glories of the labors of
our hand is God. He is the beginning and the end of all our
endeavors:

"Thus saith the LORD, Let not the wise man glory in his
wisdom, neither let the mighty man glory in his might,
let not the rich man glory in his riches: But let him that
glorieth glory in this, that he understandeth and knoweth
me, that I am the LORD which exercise lovingkindness,
judgment, and righteousness, in the earth: for in these
things I delight, saith the LORD" (Jeremiah 9:23-24).

Paul had no doubt every Christian has a gift, but he had a
concern for their proper use in the church. How the gifts are
to be communicated and used for the benefit of all was a major
concern for the apostle. Paul admonished the church to make
love the vehicle or the force behind all actions, including the
use of Spiritual gifts: "As we have therefore opportunity, let
us do good unto all men, especially unto them who are of the
household of faith" (Galatians 6:10).

This was his intention for wanting to see the saints in
Rome:

"For I long to see you, that I may impart unto you some
spiritual gift, to the end ye may be established" (Romans
1:11).

Love looks beyond individual blessing to collective blessings. Love supplies the shortage of all until there is no lack in the body. Love seeks for equality; the fullness of all men (2 Corinthians 8:14-15). As already said, the gifts are extremely valuable for the establishment of the church. They are very much needed, especially in these times of increased satanic activities - a time of great confusion, pain and distress.

Following the path of love, Paul strongly advised the church (all of us) to desire spiritual gifts. God is love, and Love is of God. Everyone that loveth is born of God (1 John 4:7), and if we love and care for another, then God dwelleth in us (1 John 4:12). If God so loved us that He sent His only begotten Son to die that we might live through Him, then we must also love God and one another.

According to the scriptures, if a man possesses all the gifts and speaking with the tongues of men and of angels, having the gift of prophecy, and understands all mysteries and all knowledge, having all faith, so that he can remove mountains, yet he has not love or do not have love as his motive, then he is nothing.

If love is not the force propelling our actions, then we have gotten it all wrong. We are like or have become as sounding brass, or a tinkling cymbal (1 Corinthians 13:1). Work of Charity without love, is no work: "And though I bestow all my goods to feed the poor, and though I give my body to be burned, and have not charity, it profiteth me nothing" (1 Corinthians 13:3):

> **"Charity never faileth: but whether there be prophecies, they shall fail; whether there be tongues, they shall cease; whether there be knowledge, it shall vanish away. For we know in part, and we prophesy in part. But when that which is perfect is come, then that which is in part shall be done away" (1 Corinthians 13:8-10).**

Love would remain because God is love. Prophesies shall fail and tongues shall cease when the Lord returns; the work of evangelism and the establishment of the individual Christian would come to fruition; they shall cease. At the time of the restoration of all things, all temporary things shall cease.

For example, spiritual gifts, marriage, the sea, and the sun would no more be needed. God Himself shall be with His people; He shall be everything to them: "There will be no more night. They will not need the light of a lamp or the light of the sun, for the Lord God will give them light. And they will reign forever and ever" (Revelation 22:5):

"And this word, Yet once more, signifieth the removing of those things that are shaken, as of things that are made, that those things which cannot be shaken may remain" (Hebrews 12:27).

When our Savior returns, He shall be glorified in us and vice versa. We shall not be able to sin. The new man shall put on the resurrected body; the new man shall have on a new body, then our salvation shall be completed. Our knowledge of Him shall be complete; we would be filled with the full knowledge of his will in all wisdom and spiritual understanding (Colossians 1:9).

However, until time, each of us must continue to study the scriptures diligently while praying and walking in the faith. We all know in part and prophecy in part, but when that which is perfect come, all imperfections shall cease. One day we shall all graduate, but for now, let us all be students and Disciples of Christ.

Further, Paul recommended that by way of love, Christians should desire the gifts and earnestly seek them, especially, those that edify the entire body, which he labeled as the best gifts. They are best because of their scope of influence, they establish or edify many.

Beware, by this statement, Paul did not intend to grade some gifts as inferior, or unimportant. He was only comparing the gifts in their wider use and wider benefits as opposed to individual or private use: "Every good and perfect gift is from above, and cometh down from the Father of lights, with whom is no variableness, neither shadow of turning" (James 1:17).

All the gifts are good because they come from the same good Lord, but the scope or overall benefits are not the same; while some may be more profitable to the individual, others may be profitable to the church:

> **"Follow after charity, and desire spiritual gifts, but rather that ye may prophesy" (1 Corinthians 14:1).**

> **"But covet earnestly the best gifts: and yet shew I unto you a more excellent way" (1 Corinthians 12:31).**

For example, he that prophesies speaks unto men to be edified, and exhorted, and comforted, but he that speaks in an unknown tongue edifies himself. In this case prophesy is of greater value because prophesy edifies many, and tongues edifies only the user:

> **"But he that prophesieth speaketh unto men to edification, and exhortation, and comfort. He that speaketh in an unknown tongue edifieth himself; but he that prophesieth edifieth the church" (1 Corinthians 14:3-4).**

The manifestations of the Spirit is given to every man, as every man hath received the gift (1 Peter 4:10). If you have not discovered yours, ask the Holy Spirit. Get busy with evangelizing; do the work of the ministry. Practically, no Christian needs a degree, a certificate, or special ordination from men, an institution or local church in order to do the work of God.

I don't think these are needed to heal the blind, lame, and the sick. Accreditations and letters of recommendations do not translate into power to save the sinner or heal the sick and neither do they promote a believer's standing before God. The best degree, I believe, is for God to know you by name and to be strengthened with might by His Spirit in the inner man:

> **"This is the word of the LORD unto Zerubbabel, saying,**

Not by might, nor by power, but by my spirit, saith the
LORD of hosts" (Zachariah 4:6).

These statements are not meant to undermine theological
education or belittle one's social standing. Follow the leading of
the Spirit and you won't be unfruitful for the Lord. Here is an
example of what the apostles of our Lord did when men were
needed for the work of the ministry:

> "Brothers, choose seven men from among you who are
> known to be full of the Spirit and wisdom. We will turn
> this responsibility over to them and will give our atten-
> tion to prayer and the ministry of the word.
>
> This proposal pleased the whole group. They chose Ste-
> phen, a man full of faith and of the Holy Spirit; also
> Philip, Procorus, Nicanor, Timon, Parmenas, and Nico-
> las from Antioch, a convert to Judaism.
>
> They presented these men to the apostles, who prayed
> and laid their hands on them. So the word of God spread.
> The number of disciples in Jerusalem increased rapidly,
> and a large number of priests became obedient to the
> faith.
>
> Now Stephen, a man full of God's grace and power, did
> great wonders and miraculous signs among the people"
> (Acts 6:3-8).

We must earnestly pray for the manifestations of the
Spiritual gifts. We must make our request known to God in
faith: "Therefore I tell you, whatever you ask for in prayer,
believe that you have received it, and it will be yours" (Mark
11:24). 'Whatever,' does not exclude spiritual gifts. After asking,
put your faith to work, practice using your gift. For example, if
you asked for the gifts of healing, go find some sick folks and tell
them to be healed in Jesus name (see example in Acts 3).

Your work is to pray for them or command the sick to be

healed in Jesus name. The work of the Spirit is to do the healing at your request. No man can charge you with practicing medicine or healing without license because, you are not the healer. Probably, the right person to be sued in court for practicing medicine without license is the Holy Spirit, undeniably, He is the healer:

> "If any of you lack wisdom, let him ask of God, that giv-eth to all men liberally, and upbraideth not; and it shall be given him. But let him ask in faith, nothing wavering. For he that wavereth is like a wave of the sea driven with the wind and tossed.
>
> For let not that man think that he shall receive any thing of the Lord. A double minded man is unstable in all his ways" (James 1:5-8).

Lack of faith, ignorance and sin may prevent a Christian from exercising the gift, but that does not mean the gift is not available to all. Sin as a virus can equally dwarf spiritual growth, create fear and doubt, destroy confidence, and witness for Christ.

Take this example, when you open a new checking account in the United States, you are given an ATM card as part of the package. The fact that you do not use the ATM card does not mean you don't have it, and neither is it the fault of the bank that you don't use the card. Contrarily, the bank would want you to use it because it is for your own convenience and for their profit as well.

This is also true with spiritual gifts. The recipient is blessed, many people are blessed, and God the giver also gets the glory. In my life, I have witnessed many cases, where believers have received the gift of the Spirit, some by laying on of hands and others while they were in private prayer.

I have heard testimonies of others who woke up from their sleep speaking in tongue. Again, the fact that one does not believe in a certain gift or the gifts does not mean God is unfaithful: "If

we believe not, yet he abideth faithful: he cannot deny himself"
(2 Timothy 2:13). The very reason that a particular gift is widely
abused or misunderstood does not also demand that it should
be discarded and demeaned.

The plausible excuse that some selected verses of scripture
dealing with this topic may be later additions, for example, Mark
16: 15-18, should not undermine their importance and prevent
their use. Another problem the church is facing concerning the
gifts are that it is being taught by people who have no clue or
experience.

Anyone who has tasted these good gifts shall never forbid
their use. Sometimes, I am amazed at men who teach and preach
on Spiritual gifts without ever experiencing any of them. How
do you teach on a phenomenon of such importance without
practical experience or manifestation? Even unbelievers agree
that the experienced teacher is the best teacher.

The knowledge of God comes to each of us through
revelation, and so are the gifts of the Spirit. Let us, therefore,
not hinder or forbid spiritual matters. I believe Spiritual gifts
should be taught, but by men who are called of God, full of
wisdom and the power of the Spirit. There is no other way
by which the church can do greater works as Jesus demanded
without the gifts of the Spirit: "Verily, verily, I say unto you,
He that believeth on me, the works that I do shall he do also;
and greater works than these shall he do; because I go unto my
Father" (John 14:12).

The great accomplishment of the early church was primarily
due to the abundant and random manifestations of these gifts
of the Spirit; it was the enablement through Spiritual gifts that
increased the church. This may be the reason the book of Acts
is also called the book of the Holy Spirit:

**"Through mighty signs and wonders, by the power of the
Spirit of God; so that from Jerusalem, and round about
unto Illyricum, I have fully preached the gospel of Christ"
(Romans 15:19).**

The gifts of the Spirit were evidenced in the life of the founder of the church Himself – Jesus Christ. He was conceived of the Holy Spirit, full of the Spirit at all times, and operated in the gifts throughout His earthly ministry:

> "And the spirit of the LORD shall rest upon him, the spirit of wisdom and understanding, the spirit of counsel and might, the spirit of knowledge and of the fear of the LORD" (Isaiah 11:2).

> "And the angel answered and said unto her, The Holy Ghost shall come upon thee, and the power of the Highest shall overshadow thee: therefore also that holy thing which shall be born of thee shall be called the Son of God" (Luke 1:35; cf. Mathew 1:20).

As already mentioned, the gifts bear witness to the scriptures; they confirm the Gospel of Christ as they are preached: "And with great power gave the apostles witness of the resurrection of the Lord Jesus: and great grace was upon them all" (Acts 4:33). They facilitate the spreading of the Gospel; they seek to confirm or authenticate the preaching of the Gospel of salvation and also the men who are called into the service of the master:

> "How shall we escape, if we neglect so great salvation; which at the first began to be spoken by the Lord, and was confirmed unto us by them that heard him; God also bearing them witness, both with signs and wonders, and with divers miracles, and gifts of the Holy Ghost, according to his own will?" (Hebrews 2:4).

> "Truly the signs of an apostle were wrought among you in all patience, in signs, and wonders, and mighty deeds" (2 Corinthians 12:12):

The manifestations of these gifts are also a sign to unbelievers. They are supposed to shift attention from men to God:

"And my speech and my preaching was not with entic-
ing words of man's wisdom, but in demonstration of the
Spirit and of power: That your faith should not stand in
the wisdom of men, but in the power of God" (1 Corinthians 2:4-5).

The harvest is plenty, but the laborers are few brethren, so
let us all get involved. The world needs Christians with a heart
and compassion for the sick and the lost (Mathew 9:37-38), and
not too many of those with fine clothes, good speeches, and fine
castles or cathedrals. There are too many egocentric Christians.
Rather, what the world needs is more of the Christocentric:

"Go ye therefore, and teach all nations, baptizing them in
the name of the Father, and of the Son, and of the Holy
Ghost: Teaching them to observe all things whatsoever I
have commanded you: and, lo, I am with you always, even
unto the end of the world. Amen" (Mathew 28:19-20).

Whereas one may not want the gifts or be bothered with
them, one must think of how many people including one's
family members could be blessed? For example, what can the
gift of healing and the working of miracles do for the brethren
who are sick? This is especially important for those terminally
ill, and those the doctors have declared incurable? One must
also think of the many praises that would rise to the throne of
God.

Have you also thought of the many praises that would rise
to the throne room of grace daily, from the lips of the many
people whose faith have been ignited, bodies healed, or have
received a word of prophesy through your gifts? Are the gifts
and fruits of the Spirit not a better way for Christ to be glorified
in and through us?

The exercises of these gifts are by no means a proof of one's
holiness (holy living), and neither are they signs of superior
spirituality. No man by his own effort can operate in Spiritual
gifts. It would be sad for any man to use the manifestations of

these gifts as a proof of acceptance and holiness; however, if the Spirit is willing to demonstrate the power of Christ through beggarly and weak vessels of those of us who believe, who are we to refuse Him? Did the scriptures not say, they are gifts of grace, unmerited and undeserving yet, God gives them to us?

This may sound apologetic, but if this is what it takes to wake up the church of Jesus Christ to the realities of our transcended livelihood, so be it. What can make the eagle afraid? Also, what can make the transcended saint who is seated with Christ in the heavenly places afraid?

What didn't our forefathers do? By these gifts they dried up whole rivers, dead bodies were raised, the sun was made to stop in its track, our Lord rose again after being in the grave for three days, and the list goes on. The times in which we live, are not for argument over the gifts, rather we must use all that is available to us to preach the good news of the Gospel to the lost before death cheats them of it.

Let us follow the example of the apostle Paul. Let us stop criticizing, judging and extricating members because of the gifts: "Some indeed preach Christ even of envy and strife; and some also of good will: "notwithstanding, every way, whether in pretence, or in truth, Christ is preached; and I therein do rejoice, yea, and will rejoice" (Philippians 1:15-18). Let us leave all judgments to the Lord, for He Himself said:

> **"Not every one that saith unto me, Lord, Lord, shall enter into the kingdom of heaven; but he that doeth the will of my Father which is in heaven. Many will say to me in that day, Lord, Lord, have we not prophesied in thy name? And in thy name have cast out devils? and in thy name done many wonderful works? And then will I profess unto them, I never knew you: depart from me, ye that work iniquity" (Mathew 7: 21-23).**

When the time is ripe, He would separate the wheat from the tares. Again, let us follow the advice of Paul to young Timothy and Peter's advice to the church:

"Till I come, give attendance to reading, to exhortation, to doctrine. Neglect not the gift that is in thee, which was given thee by prophecy, with the laying on of the hands of the presbytery" (1 Timothy 4:13-14).

The great danger to all the gifts is that they all stand the chance of being imitated, abused, and wrongly used. It is, therefore, very important that we test every spirit to see, if they are of God:

"Dear friends, do not believe every spirit, but test the spirits to see whether they are from God, because many false prophets have gone out into the world" (1 John 4:1).

Mature and Spirit-filled Christians must step up to the plate; all manifestations must be tested to ascertain the source. Not every miracle, ecstasy, or exorcism can be attributed to the Holy Spirit. Many false prophets, teachers, and miracle workers fill our churches and comb our streets today. We must, therefore, prove all things and hold fast to that which is good (1 Thessalonians 5:4). With the gift of discernment, we should be able to detect any falsehood and false Christs that may creep in to steal our soul and liberty. We must pay heed to the warnings of Jesus and the Spirit:

"Ye shall know them by their fruits. Do men gather grapes of thorns, or figs of thistles?" (Mathew 7:16, 20).

"For there shall arise false Christs, and false prophets, and shall shew great signs and wonders; insomuch that, if it were possible, they shall deceive the very elect" (Mathew 24:24).

"Beloved, believe not every spirit, but try the spirits whether they are of God: because many false prophets are gone out into the world. Hereby know ye the Spirit of God: Every spirit that confesseth that Jesus Christ is come in the flesh is of God: And every spirit that confesseth not that Jesus Christ is come in the flesh is not of God: and this is that spirit of antichrist, whereof ye have heard that it should come; and even now already is it in the world" (1 John 4:1-3).

Jesus knew full well what His regenerates would face, and before His ascension, strictly commanded His disciples to wait until they are endued with power from on high; not just any power, but the power of God. Not the power of demons or Satan, but the power of the Holy Spirit:

"But ye shall receive power, after that the Holy Ghost is come upon you: and ye shall be witnesses unto me both in Jerusalem, and in all Judaea, and in Samaria, and unto the uttermost part of the earth" (Acts 1:8).

However, understand that there are degrees of empowerment or divine enablement. Luke 24:49 may refer to the standard power which all Christians have through faith, or it may refer to the supernatural manifestation of the gifts to the degree of literally being clothed with power as one wearing a coat. Examples of such uncommon authority and power can be seen with Gideon (Judges 6:34), Samson (Judges 14:6; 16:14ff), Peter (Acts 5:15), Paul (Acts 19:11-12). This kind is very rarely seen in our days. Jesus was clothed with the power of the Spirit throughout His ministry:

"And, behold, I send the promise of my Father upon you: but tarry ye in the city of Jerusalem, until ye be endued with power from on high" (Luke 24:49).

The Gospel of Christ is the power of God to bring deliverance to prisoners of sin (Romans 1:16); it is the power of God to set the captive free. Here is the reason Jesus gave for the presence of the Spirit in His ministry: "The Spirit of the Lord is upon me, because he hath anointed me to preach the gospel to the poor; he hath sent me to heal the brokenhearted, to preach deliverance to the captives, and recovering of sight to the blind, to set at liberty them that are bruised" (Luke 4:18):

> **"How God anointed Jesus of Nazareth with the Holy Spirit and power, and how he went around doing good and healing all who were under the power of the devil, because God was with him" (Acts 10:38).**

While on earth, Jesus would not do anything outside the Spirit. Wherever He went, said and did, was done by the Spirit enablement and leadership (Mathew 4:1). Born of the Spirit, He was inseparable from the Spirit:

> **"And the angel answered and said unto her, The Holy Ghost shall come upon thee, and the power of the Highest shall overshadow thee: therefore also that holy thing which shall be born of thee shall be called the Son of God" (Luke 1:35; 4:1, 18).**

> **"And the spirit of the LORD shall rest upon him, the spirit of wisdom and understanding, the spirit of counsel and might, the spirit of knowledge and of the fear of the LORD" (Isaiah 11:2).**

> **"The Spirit of the Lord is upon me, because he hath anointed me to preach the gospel to the poor; he hath sent me to heal the brokenhearted, to preach deliverance to the captives, and recovering of sight to the blind, to set at liberty them that are bruised" (Luke 4:18).**

The coming of the Spirit was extremely important to His ministry. He explained to the disciples the necessity of returning to heaven, without which the Spirit would not come. The Spirit's coming depended upon His departure. It was to their great advantage that He departs, for then He would send to them the Spirit:

"Nevertheless I tell you the truth; It is expedient for you that I go away: for if I go not away, the Comforter will not come unto you; but if I depart, I will send him unto you" (John 16:7).

———————

"And, behold, I send the promise of my Father upon you: but tarry ye in the city of Jerusalem, until ye be endued with power from on high" (Luke 24:49).

Further, Jesus prayed purposely requesting the Father to send the disciples the Spirit. He knew the only way His redemptive work could be understood, accepted and propagated was through the Holy Spirit enablement and witness: "He shall testify of me. And ye also shall bear witness" (John 14:26-27):

"And when he is come, he will reprove the world of sin, and of righteousness, and of judgment: Of sin, because they believe not on me; of righteousness, because I go to my Father, and ye see me no more; of judgment, because the prince of this world is judged.

I have yet many things to say unto you, but ye cannot bear them now. Howbeit when he, the Spirit of truth, is come, he will guide you into all truth: for he shall not speak of himself; but whatsoever he shall hear, that shall he speak: and he will shew you things to come.

He shall glorify me: for he shall receive of mine, and shall shew it unto you. All things that the Father hath are mine: therefore said I, that he shall take of mine, and shall shew it unto you" (John 16:8-15).

Peter in his sermon on the day of Pentecost also testified that what he and his colleagues were experiencing: The ecstasy and speaking in diverse tongues was a direct fulfillment of the Savior's promise and a direct response to His request (Acts

2:33). Peter again attributed the ecstatic experiences to what
the prophet Joel spoke of many centuries before:

> "And by the hands of the apostles were many signs and
> wonders wrought among the people; (and they were all
> with one accord in Solomon's porch. And of the rest
> durst no man join himself to them: but the people mag-
> nified them.
>
> And believers were the more added to the Lord, mul-
> titudes both of men and women.) Insomuch that they
> brought forth the sick into the streets, and laid them on
> beds and couches, that at the least the shadow of Peter
> passing by might overshadow some of them. There came
> also a multitude out of the cities round about unto Jeru-
> salem, bringing sick folks, and them which were vexed
> with unclean spirits: and they were healed every one"
> (Acts 5:12-16).

> "Then Philip went down to the city of Samaria, and
> preached Christ unto them.
>
> And the people with one accord gave heed unto those
> things which Philip spake, hearing and seeing the mira-
> cles which he did.
>
> For unclean spirits, crying with loud voice, came out of
> many that were possessed with them: and many taken
> with palsies, and that were lame, were healed.
>
> And there was great joy in that city" (Acts 8:5-8; cf.
> Acts 6:8).

A great movement of the Spirit has already started on
earth, and would continue to grow until the whole earth is filled
with the glory and knowledge of the Son of God. This is not
to say everybody would become saved or Christian, but that

everybody would acknowledge in one way or the other, that Jesus Christ is the Lord:

> "And it shall come to pass in the last days, saith God, I will pour out of my Spirit upon all flesh: and your sons and your daughters shall prophesy, and your young men shall see visions, and your old men shall dream dreams:
>
> And on my servants and on my handmaidens I will pour out in those days of my Spirit; and they shall prophesy" (Acts 2:17-18).

Jesus said the manifestations of these gifts are demonstrations of the power of God over the work of Satan and demons. Again, they prove that the kingdom of God and of Christ is here and among men. Spiritual gifts are given to demonstrate the power of the kingdom into which Christians have entered and are now citizens:

> "But if I cast out devils by the Spirit of God, then the kingdom of God is come unto you" (Mathew 12:28; cf. 9:35).

There is no kingdom without power and so is the kingdom of God and of Christ. The kingdom of God (the sphere of God's rule) is set against the kingdom of the devil (the sphere of Satan's rule). The release of the former prisoners of Satan into the kingdom of God is a demonstration of the superiority of the kingdom of God: "No man can enter into a strong man's house, and spoil his goods, except he will first bind the strong man; and then he will spoil his house" (Mark 3:27; John 18:36-37).

At the moment, the kingdom of God, which is soon to come, subsists in the spiritual form in the heart of each saint: "Neither shall they say, Lo here! or, lo there! for, behold, the kingdom of God is within you" (Luke 17:21; cf. Mathew 3:2; 6:33; Luke 16:16). But, one day and very soon, the earth shall be inaugurating the physical arrival of the owner and king of the universe (Revelation 19-21).

At the moment, the church as individuals and as a collective body is included in the invisible kingdom of God on earth. There is only one church on earth, the church of which Jesus Christ is the only head and where He is recognized as the King of Kings and Lord of Lords. Physically absent, He is represented by the Holy Spirit and not by man:

> "Howbeit when he, the Spirit of truth, is come, he will guide you into all truth: for he shall not speak of himself; but whatsoever he shall hear, that shall he speak: and he will shew you things to come. He shall glorify me: for he shall receive of mine, and shall shew it unto you" (John 16:14).

> "But when the Comforter is come, whom I will send unto you from the Father, even the Spirit of truth, which proceedeth from the Father, he shall testify of me" (John 15:26).

Now, there is one particular gift that Paul wrote a whole chapter to address because of the widespread abuse, especially in the church at Corinth (1 Corinthians chapter 14). He wrote to the church asking them not to be ignorant of spiritual gifts and this commandment applies also to the church today and generations to come. This particular gift is the gift of speaking in tongues or divers kinds of tongues (1 Corinthians 12:10; 14:37). Since it has more to do with prayer, I would prefer to talk about it in the next chapter.

In conclusion, God has given to each individual Christian special gifts, abilities, or spiritual gifts by the Holy Spirit for the work of the ministry. These gifts establish the individual Christian, as well as edify the body of Christ (church). They also confirm the Gospel of salvation (Hebrews 2:4). The gifts are diverse; we don't all have the same gifts. There is power available to heal the sick, discern, prophesy, speak in tongues, etc. The Holy Spirit distributes them severally to each of us according to His own will.

Some gifts are considered best because they are most useful in the local assembly of believers, or when the church comes together for fellowship and worship. Starting from the master Jesus, the gifts have not ceased and would not, until the day of His coming. The written revelation of the scriptures has long been completed, yet we are in no way near that which is perfect, that which some bible scholars say would replace these temporary gifts.

We must earnestly desire the gifts and pray especially for the best gifts without neglecting to pray for those that establish the individual. I do not mean you should tarry or fast until you receive because that would be unnecessary. Simply, ask the Holy Spirit to show you which particular gift He has already given you or what He has made known to you either by vision, dream, and various intimations according to His own will, but be sure to ask in faith.

As you wait patiently for His response, get busy in His work, remembering the gifts are for service. Finally, I must warn you of those who desire that we be denied of this liberty also, but stand fast: "Stand fast therefore in the liberty wherewith Christ hath made us free, and be not entangled again with the yoke of bondage" (Galatians 5:1).

<u>Notes</u>

Chapter Nine

CHRISTIAN PRAYER

 Praying is one of the characteristics of a Christian. Prayer is a meaningful communication with God; it is having a conversation with God. Praying is one of the greatest and solemn moments in the life of every Christian. It is one of those rare moments when heaven unites with earth and the believer appears before the throne of grace. Before and after prayer can be as different as the night is from day for every Christian; anything can happen while a believer is in prayer. Do you remember what happened to Jesus while He was praying? His whole countenance changed: "The appearance of His face was altered, and His robe became white and glistening" (Luke 9:29).

Sometimes the presence of God can be so strong people have come out from prayer completely changed. No man can guess the results of prayer; prayer changes things, is all one can say. All things are possible for a praying believer: Prayer can move mountains, stop the sun from shinning, stop the rain from falling, silence the wind and the storm, cause a whole mountain to change places, move the sinner under contrition and repentance, and empty a full scale hospital of its sick patients by making them whole. Prayer is the believer's greatest weapon.

Prayer is the hinge on which the fruit and the gifts of the Spirit hangs. It is that which swings the door of heaven open; the means by which all requests are made to God and answers received. If the devil can stop a Christian from praying, then defeat is inevitable. Christians are advised to: "pray without ceasing" (1 Thessalonians 5:17):

"Then He spoke a parable to them, that men always ought to pray and not lose heart" (Luke 18:1).

"Watch therefore, and pray always that you may be counted worthy to escape all these things that will come to pass, and to stand before the Son of Man" (Luke 21:36).

Prayer, the word and the Spirit, are the three inseparables in the life of every believer. They are intrinsically intertwined; you can't have one without the other or two without the one. If one desires to grow spiritually and be in favor with God, then, he must have all three in his spiritual daily diet (Luke 4:4). The survival kits for every Christian are: The word which is spiritual food; prayer is the line of communication with the Spirit who is our Lord, compass, companion and comforter.

There are all kinds of prayer. Prayer could be asking, supplication, intercession, thanksgiving and petition. It is not that one has to set different times for each type of prayer; many times they happen simultaneously and unconsciously each time one is in prayer, and especially when praying in the Spirit. Some Christians prefer to write out their prayers, while others do not; however, the more you pray the more proficient and conventional prayer becomes:

"Praying always with all prayer and supplication in the Spirit, being watchful to this end with all perseverance and supplication for all the saints" (Ephesians 6:18; cf. 1 Timothy 2:1; Philippians 4:6).

"Therefore I say to you, whatever things you ask when you pray, believe that you receive them, and you will have them" (Mark 11:24).

Because of what prayer is, and does before God, it is very important that those who exercise or pray do so with all diligence, holiness, reverence, and seriousness. The prayer of each of us, regardless, can only be received and answered by grace; God in His own free will chooses to listen and answer prayer according to His own grace and mercy. Despite, we have a part to play. There are some rules to be observed.

Some may say if He receives and answers prayer by grace, why should there be rules? Rules are needed because of who He is; His nature is so pure and terrifying that nothing can approach Him without His Grace (Jesus). Once in His Grace, you become exposed to who He really is, which affects your conception, and this is what I mean by rules. You become aware that approaching God, even though by grace, demands that His word be taken seriously.

Does it mean non-believers or people of other faith or religion can't pray or approach God? That is a question only God can answer; however, according to His revealed will (the Scriptures), grace is available for every human being. Grace for non-believers is to bring them into the Truth, whereas, grace for believers is to keep them in the truth and to keep them perpetually in His presence.

Christians live by faith and faith always obeys. Hence, Christians know what it takes to open up conversation with God. They know they must approach the Holy and terrible God in holy awe and with a deep seated reverence, which transcends mere respect. Even the holy angels recognize His sway and cover their face when approaching God (Revelation 7:11):

"For the LORD your God is God of gods, and Lord of lords, a great God, a mighty, and a terrible, which regardeth not persons, nor taketh reward" (Deuteronomy 10:17).

Among the many preparations are the following. The first four are already a possession by those in union with Christ (Christians). The last two are the product of the first four and must be put on or become part of our daily walk.

Righteousness:"The sacrifice of the wicked is an abomination to the LORD, But the prayer of the upright is His delight" (Proverbs 15:8; cf. verse 29; Isaiah 1:15; 38:3; Jeremiah 7:16; 29:12; Mathew 6:5,7). "For the eyes of the Lord are over the righteous and His ears are open unto their prayers: but the face of the Lord is against them that do evil" (1 Peter 3:12). "If I regard iniquity in my heart, the Lord will not hear me" (Psalm 66:18).

Established relationship with God: "After this manner therefore pray ye: Our Father which art in heaven, Hallowed be thy name" (Mathew 6:9). "But thou, when thou prayest, enter into thy closet, and when thou hast shut thy door, pray to thy Father which is in secret; and thy Father which seeth in secret shall reward thee openly" (Mathew 6:6).

Delight in God. We must seek to please Him: "And whatsoever we ask, we receive of Him, because we keep his commandments, and do those things that are pleasing in his sight" (1 John 3:22).

We must have faith in Him: "But without faith it is impossible to please him: for he that cometh to God must believe that he is, and that he is a rewarder of them that diligently seek him" (Hebrews 11:6). It does not make sense to come to God, lacking in faith, and expect Him to do what you are asking of Him.

Living in peace with all men, especially with your spouse: "Likewise, ye husbands, dwell with them according to knowledge, giving honour unto the wife, as unto the weaker vessel, and as being heirs together of the grace of life; that your prayers be not hindered" (1Peter 3:7). In the Bible, marriage is used as an example of the type of bond that must exist between man and God. Husbands are to their wives, "even as Christ also loved the church, and gave himself for it" (Ephesians 5:25). Hence, he that cometh to God in prayer must be in perfect harmony with Jesus Christ, in order to approach God. Jesus is the only way to God; the only mediator between man and God.

Forgiven and merciful: "For if ye forgive men their trespasses, your heavenly Father will also forgive you" (6:12,14; 18:35). Again, there are various shades to prayer and different ways to communicate with God using diverse modes and postures. Just to give you a few examples from the Scriptures:

Weeping: "Now when Ezra had prayed, and when he had confessed, weeping and casting himself down before the house of God, there assembled unto him out of Israel a very great congregation of men and women and children: for the people wept very sore" (Ezra 10:1 Psalm 28:2). "Who in the days of his flesh, when he had offered up prayers and supplications with strong crying and tears unto him that was able to save him from death, and was heard in that he feared" (Hebrews 5:7).

Fasting: "And it came to pass, when I heard these words, that I sat down and wept, and mourned certain days, and fasted, and prayed before the God of heaven, And said, I beseech thee, O LORD God of heaven, the great and terrible God, that keepeth covenant and mercy for them that love him and observe his commandments" (Nehemiah 1:4-6).

Falling on your face: "And they fell upon their faces, and said, O God, the God of the spirits of all flesh, shall one man sin, and wilt thou be wroth with all the congregation?" (Numbers 16:22).

Lifting both hands towards heaven: "And Solomon stood before the altar of the LORD in the presence of all the congregation of Israel, and spread forth his hands toward heaven: And he said, LORD God of Israel, there is no God like thee, in heaven above, or on earth beneath, who keepest covenant and mercy with thy servants that walk before thee with all their heart" (1 kings 8:22,23).

Mourning: "And David lifted up his eyes, and saw the angel of the LORD stand between the earth and the heaven, having a drawn sword in his hand stretched out over Jerusalem. Then David and the elders of Israel, who were clothed in sackcloth, fell upon their faces" (1 Chronicles 21:16).

Kneeling: "O come, let us worship and bow down: let us kneel before the LORD our maker" (Psalm 95:6; Luke 22:41).

Night vigil: "Arise, cry out in the night: in the beginning of the watches pour out thine heart like water before the face of the LORD: lift up thy hands toward him for the life of thy young children, that faint for hunger in the top of every street" (Lamentations 2:19).

As for the prayers itself, there are two main forms of praying to God. Prayer, like a coin, has two sides. It is extremely important that I spend some time on this because prayer is the life-wire of every Christian. The two forms are praying with your mind or with your understanding, and the other is praying with your spirit or praying in the Holy Spirit. Both forms of prayer are good and effective and the Christian has a choice as far as method. (This is the only time the believer's newly created spirit is said to be doing something, and even then, he is logged in with the Holy Spirit):

> **What is it then? I will pray with the spirit, and I will pray with the understanding also: I will sing with the spirit, and I will sing with the understanding also" (1 Corinthians 14:15).**

A Christian can pray, sing songs of praises and adore God using his own choice of language and words. This we call praying with the understanding or mind. He can do the same thing using the language and words given to him directly by the Holy Spirit (language and words unknown and never learned). This also is called praying with spirit.

Praying with the understanding

Every Christian has a choice when it comes to prayer to use the language and words of choice in communicating with God. Sometimes, Christians learn the words of prayer from books including the Bible, and also from one another, especially as we hear other people pray. Other times, we pray as moved by the Spirit, expressing deep spiritual truths yet using our own language and words.

When praying with your understanding, you pray in a known language; a language you know, understand and probably have learned. You control the choice of words, phrases and sentences, and duration, though not in all cases. The time spent in prayer differs with individual Christians. Some pray long, and others short; some pray all the time, and others rarely pray.

Sometimes, praying with understanding can become very hard because of distractions. Mind wandering is one of the enemies of this form of praying. Sometimes it is hard to stay focused, especially when the body is tired or when the mind is under stress. Another enemy is sleep; the tendency to fall asleep during prayer. To solve this problem, many Christians resort to liturgical methods or write down the whole prayer and read them to God.

There is no problem with that, but if you remember what prayer is: "A conversation with your heavenly Father," then you want to avoid sounding liturgical; you want to be able to freely express your feelings, adorations, devotion, and needs to your own heavenly Father. But if this is what works best for you, then keep it up. When prayer is spontaneous, it is beautiful and pleasurable, and I believe we must learn to pray this way. Then prayer becomes conversational and enjoyable.

It is possible even to lose the consciousness of time when prayers become part of you. God is not a language teacher watching over your words for grammar and spelling mistakes. Feel free to communicate openly and confidently by faith with your Father. It doesn't matter how you start, what language is used, and how you end. As long as you remember to start or approach the Father at all times and under all circumstances in the name of Jesus, and end in the same name, you are fine:

"Giving thanks always for all things unto God and the Father in the name of our Lord Jesus Christ" (Ephesians 5:20):

"And whatsoever ye do in word or deed, do all in the name of the Lord Jesus, giving thanks to God and the Father by him" (Colossians 3:20).

Confession of known and unknown sins is always part of Christian prayer. We cannot underestimate or ignore the Father's hatred for sin, but if we confess and forsake our sins; "he is faithful and just to forgive us our sins, and to cleanse us from all unrighteousness" (1 John 1:9).

The right and best way of praying with the understanding is to let the Spirit guide you. Even though you get to choose the language and the words, it is important to be in tune with the Spirit. Expect the Spirit to take over somewhere along the time of praying.

This is not a rule, but you can, for example, start in the name of Jesus, follow through with confession of sins, even if you are not aware or convicted of any, and then, continue with praises. This could be the Psalms, hymns, your own words of adoration, songs of praise, etc., and believe it or not, the Spirit of God would take over the prayer.

To be a student of prayer, you must be a student of the bible. You must constantly read your bible. In this way, you build up a biblical vocabulary. The more your knowledge of the word, the more the Spirit feeds your mind with scriptures as you pray. You will be able to effectively pray in accordance to God's will, and to His pleasure; prayer becomes a sweet-smelling fragrance to the Lord.

Another way to learn how to pray, is to pray with other bible believing and praying Christians; remember the saying, iron sharpens iron:

"Let the word of Christ dwell in you richly in all wisdom; teaching and admonishing one another in psalms and hymns and spiritual songs, singing with grace in your hearts to the Lord" (Colossians 3:16).

When we allow the Spirit to guide and lead our Christian life, He does not only teach us the word of God, but He also helps us with our prayers. The Spirit is our teacher in everything. The Spirit guides us through the different stages of prayer; we cry, shout, jump, intercede, petition, give thanks, and meditate as the Spirit leads:

"Likewise the Spirit also helpeth our infirmities: for we know not what we should pray for as we ought: but the Spirit itself maketh intercession for us with groanings which cannot be uttered" (Romans 8:26).

Jesus taught us how to pray after the disciples had Him to. They had witnessed the prayer life of the master and then wanted to follow His example. Jesus did not hesitate to give them the prayer model which we call the Lord's Prayer:

"After this manner therefore pray ye: Our Father which art in heaven, Hallowed be thy name. Thy kingdom come, Thy will be done in earth, as it is in heaven. Give us this day our daily bread. And forgive us our debts, as we forgive our debtors. And lead us not into temptation, but deliver us from evil: For thine is the kingdom, and the power, and the glory, for ever. Amen" (Mathew 6:9-13).

In this prayer model, we see the following progression:

1. We see our relationship (with our heavenly father); and how to worship (hallowed be thy name). Prayer is a line of communication: It is private conversation between a Christian and his heavenly Father. Christians worship the Father for all of His grace and mercy; past, present and future.

2. Oneness in purpose (thy will be done on earth, as it is in heaven). Thy will be done, if accepted, is the summary of all prayer requests. It is all that a believer needs and must ask for himself, his family and the world.

3. Dependence (give us this day our daily bread). Daily reminder of total dependence for all spiritual, physical, and material needs. Faith in the promises of God is a believer's way of life. Tithes and offering is a Christian's access into the treasury of heaven; His death for the salvation of his soul and stripes for the healing of his body.

4. Repentance, reciprocity, and gratitude (forgive us our debts as we forgive our debtors). The same measure, we measure unto others, shall be measured unto us and this applies to all the actions of a man. This measure is a universal law and applies to all; Christians and non-Christians.

5. Guidance and protection (lead us not into temptation, but deliver us from evil). The Lord is every Christian's strong tower, fortress, and deliverer. Since the life of every Christian is hid in Christ in God, there is no need for fear. Each of us can confidently live each day knowing that we are protected by the Father and by a host of His angels.

6. Submission, acknowledgement and praise (for thine is the kingdom, the power, and the glory, for ever. Amen). Sanctification, which is the renewal of the Christian mind by the Holy Spirit, is in knowing that you are holy or dead to sin. It is also a daily progression of the true knowledge of God our Savior. This knowledge translates into joy, praises, and adorations in the life of a Christian; it is a fountain that rises each day in the soul in honor of all the works of God.

PRAYING IN THE SPIRIT

Praying in the Holy Spirit is the other side of the praying coin as mentioned earlier. This kind of prayer is transcended; it is a miracle. Ninety five percent of the time, the Christian praying in this way is not privileged to know the content and language being used. The Bible calls this prayer language, 'unknown tongue' or simply, praying in tongue. Like Paul, a Christian can pray with the spirit, and sing with the spirit. This is only possible through the Holy Spirit or through the Spirit's enablement; one cannot pray this kind of prayer on his own":

> **"For if I pray in an unknown tongue, my spirit prayeth, but my understanding is unfruitful" (1 Corinthians 14:14)**

When praying with the spirit, the mind is unfruitful, which means the words of the prayer are not the product of the mind understanding. The human mind takes a break. In fact, this is one of the fundamental uniqueness of the transcended life. To be given the ability to pray in a language never learnt or unknown to you, is a phenomenon; this is a supernatural manifestation, it is a miracle. This may be the only time a man can communicate intelligently with his Maker outside his mind; without the use of his mental faculty. It is a mystery:

> **"For he that speaketh in an unknown tongue speaketh not unto men, but unto God: for no man understandeth him; howbeit in the spirit he speaketh mysteries. For if I pray in an unknown tongue, my spirit prayeth, but my understanding is unfruitful" (1 Corinthians 14:2).**

Praying with the spirit, the Spirit chooses the words and the language on behalf of the believer. This is a perfect example of a believer's oneness with the Spirit. Even though, in most cases, we are not privileged to understand what is being said, there is absolute peace within; our spirit is in perfect agreement with the Holy Spirit:

"For what man knoweth the things of a man, save the spirit of man which is in him? Even so the things of God knoweth no man, but the Spirit of God" (1 Corinthians 2:11).

We cooperate with the Spirit by releasing our mouth for His use and for our profit. Our human spirit says amen to all that the Spirit prays on our behalf:

"Likewise the Spirit also helpeth our infirmities: for we know not what we should pray for as we ought: but the Spirit itself maketh intercession for us with groanings which cannot be uttered. And he that searcheth the hearts knoweth what is the mind of the Spirit, because he maketh intercession for the saints according to the will of God." (Romans 8:26-27).

When a Christian prays with or in an unknown tongue, he is praying to God; it is the believer's other private and direct line through the Holy Spirit (the first being through the mind). This line never goes wrong, gets busy, tapped into or boggled by a third party. Except by permission, and enablement by the Spirit to understand and interpret, this line remains closed and a mystery.

This is the uniqueness of the existing relationship between the Father and each of His sons or children. This particular gift is for the spiritual building up of oneself; it is for the establishment of the individual Christian:

"He that speaketh in an unknown tongue edifieth himself" (1 Corinthians 14:4).

Because the mind is free when this gift is in use, Christians while praying can engage the mind in other things. For an example, they can pray while cooking, driving (of course with eyes opened), doing the laundry or even studying and yet, be perfectly normal. Using this gift, the Christian can pray all day and not feel exhausted or short of words.

Paul, writing to the church in Corinth, told them he prays in tongues more than any of them. He made this statement while addressing the enthused church about their abuse of the gift of tongues:

"I thank my God, I speak with tongues more than ye all" (1 Corinthians 14:18).

I guess this is one of the secrets of Paul's fervency and dynamism in the work of the ministry. Prayer changes things and people. Heaven pays attention when a believer is in prayer. Prayer is health to the soul; the perfect antidote for stress and worry.

Whenever we come together as a praying church, we must expect wonderful things to happen. I have been to meetings where it has been difficult even to go home or close the service because of the presence of the Lord. It is amazing and a joy to watch the display of the multiple gifts of the Spirit among believers.

It is a blessing to be in a service where the Spirit is fully at work and where the gifts of each member are synchronized for the good of all. I have been in services where believers have remained slain in the Spirit for hours, others literally unable to move from their seat or standing position. Some remained glued to the floor while singing and making melody in their heart.

Many new songs over the centuries have come out of Holy Ghost revivals (name given by some for services where the gifts are at work). Wherever the gifts are being manifested, there is definitely the presence of God:

"Speaking to yourselves in psalms and hymns and spiritual songs, singing and making melody in your heart to the Lord" (Ephesians 5:19).

The freedom to choose which form to use in prayer is a great asset to Christians, especially for those who desire to spend more time in prayer. Sometimes I wonder why we have so many songs recorded from our understanding and not one song from our spirit.

I believe the world would be blessed if we could get some tongue speaking songs on tape. Who knows what a blessing that could bring to our homes as they are played over the airwaves? It might serve a better purpose than some of the mind destroying hard core music that has captivated most children.

Can tongue praying be taught? No. Can it be imitated? Yes, but to what avail? Tongue is not the language of men. Tongue is speaking to God and not to men, so it does not make sense to imitate. Like the smoke from a burning bush, imitated prayer rises into the sky and then falls back to the ground. Nothing is more damnable than to make mockery of the things of God. To flee from sin is understanding:

"The fear of the Lord is the beginning of wisdom: and the knowledge of the holy is understanding" (Proverbs 9:10).

It is not expedient for any local congregation to forbid speaking in tongues; rather, it must be encouraged. When individual Christians are established, the collective body is also established. After all, a church is made of individuals. The leadership must teach and make room for the operations and manifestations of the gifts of the Spirit. By so doing, we would be building a healthy and a well balanced church. The body is better served when the diverse and dynamic spiritual gifts are encouraged for the course of Christ.

Further, it is expedient for those with the gift of tongue to pray for the gift of interpretation (1 Corinthians 14:13). Tongues' speaking is a blessing whenever believers assemble for fellowship:

"Wherefore, brethren, covet to prophesy, and forbid not to speak with tongues" (1 Corinthians 14:39)

Sometimes, in the church, the Spirit grants the leave for part of tongue communications to be understood. This normally falls under the gift of prophecy, or becomes gift of prophesy in manifestation. Remember, the gifts have one source and one purpose; hence, in many ways linked. Therefore, changing from one gift to another is not a problem. The Spirit can do whatever He wants with His gifts at any given assembly of believers.

When the gift of tongue is in use in the assembly of the saints without accompanying interpretation, no man understands what is being said, and therefore becomes unfruitful. Tongue speaking is a sign for believers and as already mentioned, establishes the individual directly, but the body indirectly. However, it's proper place and usefulness is in the personal prayer life of the believer and not in the assembly of the saints.

In the church, as our Brother Paul has taught us, the use must be limited and channeled for the benefit of all those assembled. For example, tongue is a prayer going up to God; prophesy is a word coming down from God. Hence, if there is proper order and knowledge of the gifts in the worship service of the church, both can be worked out decently. The leadership would know when to pause in the worship, which is going up to receive a message from God which is coming down.

On the other hand, if a message is communicated in tongue, there should be an interpreter; otherwise, the person must be quieted and the worship service continued:

> **"How is it then, brethren? when ye come together, every one of you hath a psalm, hath a doctrine, hath a tongue, hath a revelation, hath an interpretation. Let all things be done unto edifying"** (1 Corinthians 14:26).

All things must be done orderly and decently in the assembly of the saints (1 Corinthians 14:40).

Beloved, these things I am writing to you are not my personal views or my own opinion about supernatural gifts, for no prophecy of scripture is of any private interpretation. All I am doing is presenting to you and all who care to read this book, the truth as laid down in scripture. And if any still lack understanding, let him ask of God, if these things be true or not (James 1:5).

Prayer is powerful; it is medicine for the soul. God has gifted His church with many spiritual blessings for the believer's establishment. What each of us needs in this life and for godliness are already provided by God and can be received through prayer.

God has given us Jesus Christ, His only beloved Son. He has also given us His Holy Spirit to dwell with and in us. The Spirit has made available to the church all kinds of spiritual gifts; supernatural gifts to be used in the life of the saint and in service of our Lord. It is up to each of us to decide what to do with all that is freely and graciously given.

Prayer is a must for all Christians. If we want to pray only with our understanding, then fair and good, but if we also decide, in addition, to use the gift of tongues, it is best. Paul said, it is best to pray with both the spirit and with the understanding. However, in the church or in the assembly of the saints, let us beware, and do that which is right and to the benefit of all.

Speaking in an unknown tongue is one of the many supernatural gifts. Each of the gifts has their proper place, use or function. I bring out this point because very often Christians misuse the gifts. Often you come across a Christian praying for the sick using the gift of tongue instead of the gifts of healing. It appears that unknown tongue is in many ways used as a substitute for all the other gifts, but this ought not to be.

If it is about the healing of the sick, let us be humble enough to call in the brethren who have the appropriate gift to do the job. This will save time and energy and will produce better results. In the local church, this counsel is very important. Often times, the pastor is looked upon as the person having all the gifts. He is the person to pray for sick, prophesy, and have the word of knowledge etc., while the rest of the congregations are only recipients or spectators.

Notwithstanding, those who evangelize and preach the Gospel to the unsaved seem to enjoy special privileges because of the promise attached: "Go ye into all the world, and preach the Gospel to every creature. And these signs shall follow them that believe." Any believer who engages in street evangelism is bound to see the Spirit at work. Jesus is glorified as the Spirit chooses the appropriate gift to meet the various needs of the hearers. It is really a joy to evangelize and to see souls saved and healed. Try it.

In conclusion, a Christian can pray with the understanding and also with the spirit. Both methods are effective and useful, especially when the Spirit is in control. A Christian is under no obligation to speak in unknown tongue. It is a matter of choice, but it does not hurt to taste (experience) this gift before rejection. The Spirit can give it to you, but the decision to use it is yours.

Prayer, whether with the understanding or with the spirit, is not a choice. Christians don't choose to pray, we are commanded to pray. There are many kinds of prayer; intercession, thanksgiving, worship, petition, and many more. Prayer is not just asking for things to consume on the flesh, it could be serious groaning for Spiritual insight or a deepening petition for a closer walk with God. It is the duty of every Christian to pray without ceasing (cf. 1 Thessalonians 5:17).

<u>Notes</u>

Chapter Ten

MAGNIFICENT GRACE

Now, let us talk about something wonderful, glorious and gracious and that is, the grace of God. There is nothing more precious to man (believer and non-believer), than the grace of God. If it were possible for a man to sell the whole world for the grace of God, it would utterly be contempt and condemned. Grace is the one word that sums up all that God, who became man, is to fallen humanity.

Nothing is greater and more enduring than the grace of God. It is the sea in which love and faith find their proper places (1 Timothy 1:14). The finite mind is incapable of searching the depth, beauty, bountifulness, and the free heartedness of God. Grace is the one word that says it all.

The best state any being on earth can be, at any moment in time, whether they are on the earth or in heaven, is to be in or under the grace of God. Grace is the basis for all the blessings of God towards His creatures. Election, justification, sanctification, Christian liberty, spiritual gifts and the gifts of men to the church are all derivatives of grace. As a matter of fact, all the benevolences of God to mankind in general come as a result of grace. Christianity from start to finish is grace:

"For the LORD God is a sun and shield: the LORD will give grace and glory: no good thing will he withhold from them that walk uprightly" (Psalm 84:11)

Does anybody want to know how God can forget a multitude of sins yet remember the number of hairs on our head? The resounding answer is grace. Grace makes the poor rich, frees the captive, and turns shame into glory, dishonor to honor, faithless to faith, unthankful to thankfulness, enmity to friendship, hatred to love and the diseased to wholeness. It changes the course of hell bound sinners to heaven bound saints. Grace seeks that which was lost and repairs the broken (Luke 19:10; cf. Mathew 4:23-25; Luke 4:18; Acts 20:24). Grace is magnificent because it comes from the magnificent God. God is gracious: ". . . when he crieth unto me, that I will hear; for I am gracious" (Exodus 22:27; cf. 1 Peter 5:10). Grace can only be received as a gift from the gracious God who is kind, longsuffering, patient and merciful (Nehemiah 9:17).

Grace is free because it is priceless; no creature can merit the grace of God. It cannot be earned. It is antithesis to works the two being mutually exclusive. When you work you get paid, but this is not the case with God's grace; one cannot work and get paid by grace. There are no merits in grace; everything in grace is free; grace is transcendent:

"Now to him that worketh is the reward not reckoned of grace, but of debt" (Romans 4:4).

I am not expecting you to ask me to define God's grace because the definition of grace is beyond the scope of mortal intelligence. It would be like asking me to drink all the waters of the ocean. Nevertheless, before I give you the biblical definition, let me with the help of the Lord.

Grace is God and God is grace, in the same way God is Love and Love is God (1 John 4:8). Grace can be rightly labeled as one of God's eternal attributes. Grace is the willingness of God to extend His love, power and all that He is. God's grace is personified in His Son Jesus Christ. Jesus is the grace of God; from Him, every man receives the grace of God. God gave us grace, Jesus bought it for us, and His Spirit makes it available to every man:

> **"For the law was given by Moses, but grace and truth came by Jesus Christ"** (John 1:17).

> **"And of his fulness have all we received, and grace for grace"** (John 1:16).

The grace of God embraces all of the following: Favor, joy, acceptance, kindness, gratitude, thankfulness, favor done without expectation, kindly treated, pleasantly dealt with, unmerited love. Grace is the good news of the Gospel of Christ (Acts 20:24). Grace is the home of all those who are redeemed:

> **"By whom also we have access by faith into this grace wherein we stand, and rejoice in hope of the glory of God"** (Romans 5:2; 6:14,15).

Grace transcends human compassion and pity; it is infinitely boundless and unsearchable. In fact, Grace is much more appreciated, when the difference between a sinner and a saint is well understood. The voice of grace is louder than the violent clashes of the ocean waters and the angry noise of thunder and lightning, despite, its voice is still and clear.

Here are some of the speeches of grace: "Come unto me, all ye that labour and are heavy laden and I will give you rest" (Mathew 11:28). "Ho, every one that thirsteth, come ye to the waters, and he that hath no money; come ye, buy, and eat; yea, come, buy wine and milk without money and without price. "Come now, and let us reason together, saith the LORD: though your sins be as scarlet, they shall be as white as snow; though they be red like crimson, they shall be as wool" (Isaiah 1:18). "But God commendeth his love toward us, in that, while we were yet sinners, Christ died for us. Are all these not gracious words? A healing to the broken hearted and a rest for the weary soul?

The Bible has the following definition; in summary:

"But after that the kindness and love of God our Saviour toward man appeared, not by works of righteousness which we have done, but according to his mercy he saved us, by the washing of regeneration, and renewing of the Holy Ghost" (Titus 3:4-5).

There cannot be salvation or justification without grace: "Even when we were dead in sins, hath quickened us together with Christ, (by grace ye are saved): "For by grace are ye saved through faith; and that not of yourselves: it is the gift of God" (Ephesians 2:5, 8). Grace makes all things ennobling and even enviable. Grace produces thunderous praise from the lips of all beneficiaries, and gracious response from all recipients:

"Even when we were dead in sins, hath quickened us together with Christ, (by grace ye are saved. For by grace are ye saved through faith; and that not of yourselves: it is the gift of God" (Ephesians 2:5,8).

Grace knows no classification. It is the same for every man; the same measure for all, invited, and welcomed without preconditions. No man can work into grace but, every man can work from grace. Works done from salvation do follow us to the judgment seat of Christ (Revelations 13:14): "For we must all appear before the judgment seat of Christ; that every one may receive the things done in his body, according to that he hath done, whether it be good or bad" (2 Corinthians 5:10). Under grace human efforts and creations deserve no merits:

"Even so then at this present time also there is a remnant according to the election of grace. And if by grace, then is it no more of works: otherwise grace is no more grace. But if it be of works, then it is no more grace: otherwise work is no more work" (Romans 11:5-6).

"Who hath saved us, and called us with an holy calling, not according to our works, but according to his own purpose and grace, which was given us in Christ Jesus before the world began" (2 Timothy 1:9).

Let me give you some powerful examples of what grace can do. The first mention of this gracious word was in relation to Noah: "But Noah found grace in the eyes of the LORD" (Genesis 6:8). Noah, like the rest of the people of his generation would have perished in the flood if not for the grace he found in the sight of God. His own uprightness or integrity could not have prevented him from drowning under the flood.

Israel is another example of what happens to a people or nation which finds favor with God. From Egypt to Canaan to our present day, no man can measure God's gracious attitude towards Israel. The numerous times Jehovah God delivered them from their enemies and from extinction, and the abundant blessings Jehovah has showered on them to date. Grace chose Israel and set them apart from the rest of the world in the same way it is choosing Jews and Gentiles into the church today.

What separated Israel as the special people of God was not their good works, but the grace of God. Here is what Moses said: "For wherein shall it be known here that I and thy people have found grace in thy sight? Is it not in that thou goest with us? So shall we be separated, I and thy people, from all the people that are upon the face of the earth" (Exodus 33:16; cf. Ezra 9:8). The same grace will save all Israel when the Messiah returns (Revelations 7).

The early disciples were both chosen and enabled by the Holy Spirit to perform great miracles because of the grace of God that was upon them:

"And with great power gave the apostles witness of the resurrection of the Lord Jesus: and great grace was upon them all" (Acts 4:33).

Further, the marvels of the Christian calling, how certain individuals from all walks of life, irrespective of race, color, and gender are elected and made into the people of God is all by grace. Christians everywhere are living examples of what grace can do; how grace can turn former sinners and unbelievers into saints, and not only that, but also preserve them holy before the Holy God perpetually (Romans 3:24; Ephesians 2:4).

Spiritual gifts and the calling of individual gifted Christians for leadership and service in the church are all by grace. For example, to be chosen as a pastor or teacher in the body of Christ is purely by grace:

> **"For I say, through the grace given unto me, to every man that is among you, not to think of himself more highly than he ought to think; but to think soberly, according as God hath dealt to every man the measure of faith" (Romans 12:3; cf. Galatians 1:15).**

God in Christ saves us by grace, preserves us by grace (Jude 1:1), and would glorify us by grace (Romans 5:1-2 cf. 3:24,28; 11:5). Every day that we live on God's earth is by grace including the provisions of food, clothing, and shelter:

> **"Even so then at this present time also there is a remnant according to the election of grace" (Romans 11:5; cf. Romans 4:16).**

Christian service whether to fellow man or God is by grace: "Wherefore we receiving a kingdom which cannot be moved, let us have grace, whereby we may serve God acceptably with reverence and godly fear" (Hebrews 12:28). We are children of God and joint heirs with Christ by grace (1 Peter 3:7).

Each and every individual Christian is directly responsible to God. God has no grandchildren. There is only one Father, that is our maker and all Christians are His children: "And call no man your father upon the earth: for one is your Father, which is in heaven" (Mathew 23:9; 1 John 3:1).

As mentioned earlier, grace stands opposed to the law which worketh wrath, the two being mutually exclusive. The law condemns; grace pardons and acquits:

"Christ is become of no effect unto you, whosoever of you are justified by the law; ye are fallen from grace" (Galatians 2:16; 5:4).

Grace is the remedy for sin, yet the two are antagonistic to each other. Sin pays wages - the wages of death. Grace gives life and life in abundance (Romans 5:20; 6:1, 15). Grace asks no question, it is void of all that is legal and conventional. The grace of God regenerates sinners into saints, the unrighteous to righteous, and the unholy to holiness.

To be under God's grace is great. Can you imagine saying to someone no matter what you do God is with you. Yet, this statement is very true of grace. This is exactly what grace is and says. But does this statement not sound like license to sin? God forbid.

Grace to the ignorant and spiritually immature may sound like a license to sin; after all, I am going to heaven on the merit of Christ; what difference does it make weather I sin or not, they say. To the mature and God fearing, on the other hand, grace is an opportunity to live a gracious life and to live a life of holiness.

Grace is not a license to sin, but the remedy for sin. Grace abhors sin; no Christian can hide under the cloak of grace to sin. "This I say then, Walk in the Spirit, and ye shall not fulfill the lust of the flesh" is a command for every Christian to obey:

"What shall we say, then? Shall we go on sinning so that grace may increase? God forbid" (Romans 6:1, 2).

God is gracious and He desires that each of His children enjoy His grace. No Christian is outside the grace of the kind and merciful God. All things are possible under God's grace. In grace, a Christian can fall seven times, but shall rise seven times. Under the grace of God we can turn mourning into dancing and captivity into freedom.

In conclusion, the grace of God is the reason for Christian liberty and life in the Spirit. We are called and saved not according to our works, but according to His purpose and grace. This grace was given to us in Christ Jesus even before the world began. So beloved, while we have this grace and mercy, let us enjoy every bit of it. Let us enjoy our relationship with our Savior and God and with one another; for this is the believers' portion in this life. Further, we must not allow sin to cripple or weigh us down. If in case we sin, let us be prompt to confess for the blood of Jesus is available to cleanse us from all sins; there is abundant grace and mercy to grant immediate forgiveness.

Further still, if there is no sin, do not create one. Just keep yourself unspotted and blameless before God and avoid repetitive confessions of sins past and present. The moment sin is confessed, accept God's forgiveness and move on. Faith is a product of grace and with your faith in the faith of the Son of God you can sour high over every mountain of obstacles with wings like the eagle. The last verse in the book of Revelation says to all believers: "The grace of our Lord Jesus Christ be with you all," and let all Christians say, Amen (Revelation 22:21).

Chapter Eleven

FAITH

Everything about the new man is glorious; born a spiritual being, his way of life transcends the natural. The way the new man lives and does business is quite different; it is out of the ordinary. Living in two realms; the spiritual and the natural, faith is his way of life for each individual Christian.

Faith is a gift from God; the first gift in the line of gifts. There is only one place to find faith, and that is in the Gospel of Christ. Faith is enablement; it is the power to live the kind of life expected of the sons of God:

"For we walk by faith, not by sight" (2 Corinthians 5:6).

Faith is the confident trust in unseen power of God; through faith, objective reality is not necessary. Daily life is lived through the Spirit who is invisible. God's Spirit produces a conviction in us of things not seen; that they actually exist:

"Now faith is the substance of things hoped for, the evidence of things not seen" (Hebrews 11:2).

Faith seals off self; faith abandons all self-reliance, and trusting only in God. Faith is being sure and certain about unseen realities and hope. A Christian uses his natural senses to relate and to live out his natural life. In the same vein, he uses his faith to relate and to live out his spiritual life. For example, a Christian can present his resume for a particular job, but he does not rely on the resume to get the job, he relies on faith through prayer. The resume may not even bear any relevance to the job applied, but for the Christian heaven has the final say in all things.

Unbelief is man's greatest enemy, but faith is his greatest asset; when faith goes, everything goes. Faith is the very opposite of unbelief. The Old Testament fathers obtained a good report from God because of their faith (Hebrews 11:2). They pleased God by trusting His word with their whole heart:

"But without faith it is impossible to please him: for he that cometh to God must believe that he is, and that he is a rewarder of them that diligently seek him" (Hebrews 11:6).

Life is lost without faith in God; life is a gift from God and is sustained by total trust in the word of the living God. Christianity without faith is no Christianity; likewise, faith without Christianity is no faith. The life of a Christian from start to finish is faith; each of us is justified, sanctified, sustained, preserved, and protected, and shall be glorified:

"The just shall live by his faith" (Habakkuk 2:4).

Faith is total trust in everything God says; faith says yes to every word that cometh from the mouth of God without question or doubt. Breaking the law of God is not the smartest thing to do. This can only happen when one loses faith in God. For example, Adam broke God's word when he believed Satan's lies, and when Satan maligned the word of God. But what did Adam gain by his action? Nothing, instead he lost everything and finally died because of his disobedience to the word of God.

Every man's survival depends on his obedience to the word of God. Disobedience and obedience to the word of God determines every man's fate. Man without faith in God's word is considered dead. However, faith in the word of God is life and life in abundance to all who choose to obey. Since it is absolutely impossible for God to lie, His word must be trusted and obeyed. Man is finite and fallible, but God is infinite, pure, and infallible; His word is forever sure:

"Man shall not live by bread alone, but by every word that proceedeth out of the mouth of God" (Mathew 4:4).

God is the very essence of man's existence; His Word is the life of every man. We live to eat and not vice versa. Man's diet is not just bread or food, but essentially the word of God. The greatest evil that can happen to any man is to be rich in the eyes of men, but not rich before God; to be materially rich, but spiritually poor toward God. Life comes before wealth; each of us must live before we can create wealth. It is for this reason Jesus admonished mankind to first seek the kingdom of God.

God is the length of days for every man (Deuteronomy 30:20). If any man wishes to enjoy endless life and happiness, then faith in God is the road. What is the use of riches without life? Or, what good is more money without eternal life? Ask the ancient, and they would tell you, all the labor of man under the sun is vanity upon vanity without faith in God. Here is a story as told by Jesus to drive home this very important point:

"There was a certain rich man, which was clothed in purple and fine linen, and fared sumptuously every day:

And there was a certain beggar named Lazarus, which was laid at his gate, full of sores, and desiring to be fed with the crumbs which fell from the rich man's table: moreover the dogs came and licked his sores.

And it came to pass, that the beggar died, and was carried by the angels into Abraham's bosom: the rich man also died, and was buried; and in hell he lift up his eyes, being in torments, and seeth Abraham afar off, and Lazarus in his bosom. And he cried and said, Father Abra-

ham, have mercy on me, and send Lazarus, that he may dip the tip of his finger in water, and cool my tongue; for I am tormented in this flame.

But Abraham said, Son, remember that thou in thy life-time receivedst thy good things, and likewise Lazarus evil things: but now he is comforted, and thou art tor-mented" (Mathew 16:19-25).

To live as a Christian is to live a lifestyle of total dependence on God. Faith comes to each of us through the Gospel of grace. Another name for Christianity is 'the faith' (Colossians 2:7; 1Timothy 1:2). Faith is not something that man can produce or develop on his own; it can only be given by God. Think of faith as the passage through which all the blessings of God in Christ flows to the Christian. The Holy Spirit connects each of us to the main source which is Jesus, and keeps us connected to keep the supply line open. This is one of the reasons dependence on the Spirit for the Christian is indispensable:

For in it the righteousness of God is revealed from faith to faith; as it is written, "The just shall live by faith." (Romans 1:17; cf. Galatians 3:11).

When a man's ways please the Lord, he can ask whatever he wants from Him and it shall be granted. God has already given us all that we need for this life and for godliness, but even if that is not enough, He is willing to give us more if only we ask in faith. We are guaranteed answers to all requests, if we ask in total obedience and trust. Our faith must not be different from Jesus faith in God. The faith of Jesus is the God kind of faith and each of us is expected to exhibit His kind of faith in our daily walk with God:

"And Jesus answering saith unto them, Have faith in God. For verily I say unto you, That whosoever shall say unto this mountain, Be thou removed, and be thou cast into the sea; and shall not doubt in his heart, but shall believe that those things which he saith shall come to pass; he shall have whatsoever he saith" (Mark 11:22-23; Luke 14:1).

Faith in the finished work of Jesus is what saved us; it would take His faith to keep us daily in God's approval. Each of us is expected to live out our daily Christian life in the same way that we became saved; in the same way Jesus lived while on earth. Christians must live a life of total dependence on God's word. The end of your faith is the salvation of your soul; this means you will not be disappointed if you do, God will bring you to an expected end:

"As ye have therefore received Christ Jesus the Lord, so walk ye in him" (Colossians 2:6).

Some Christians aspire to be like David, Abraham, Katherine Kuhlman, Charles Finney, Charles Wesley etc; because they have admirable qualities in the way they led their Christian lives. God, on one hand, does not want us to be like any of them because they all had human flaws: "For there is not a just man upon earth, that doeth good, and sinneth not" (Ecclesiastes 7:20). Rather, God expects each of us, including them, to be like Jesus. Jesus is man's only role model.

Further, none of us needs their faith because they were all of limited faith; instead, each of us needs our own faith from God; for God to grow in us His own kind of faith. As we allow ourselves to be changed by the Holy Spirit from glory to glory and we become more and more like Jesus, we develop His kind of faith (the God kind of faith).

"I am crucified with Christ: nevertheless I live; yet not I, but Christ liveth in me: and the life which I now live in the flesh I live by the faith of the Son of God, who loved me, and gave himself for me" (Galatians 2:20).

Paul was content to live by the faith of the Son of God. For him, his livelihood and victories rested on Him; what his

Savior had already done and earned on his behalf. For example, as far as he was concerned, Jesus death and resurrection were his death and resurrection; His faith and victories were his faith and victories. He lived daily to know him and to be conformed into His likeness and image. But, believe it or not, Paul's story is the story of every Christian. Jesus died for every man, so that those who live, might live together with Him and for Him (cf. 1 Thessalonians 5:10):

> "For none of us liveth to himself, and no man dieth to himself. For whether we live, we live unto the Lord; and whether we die, we die unto the Lord: whether we live therefore, or die, we are the Lord's" (Romans 14:7-8).

> "For the love of Christ constraineth us; because we thus judge, that if one died for all, then were all dead: And that he died for all, that they which live should not henceforth live unto themselves, but unto him which died for them, and rose again" (2 Corinthians 5:15).

Satan would bow to every believer who walks in the faith of Jesus; when Satan knows that you know he was defeated on the cross. The same is true before God; God recognizes each individual Christian victorious, successful, and more than a conqueror in His Son: "Examine yourselves, whether ye be in the faith; prove your own selves. Know ye not your own selves, how that Jesus Christ is in you, except ye be reprobates?" (2 Corinthians 13:5).

Every Christian has the approval of Jesus to use His name to destroy or overcome the works of the devil. It is up to each of us to make Satan know that we know and he would flee from us. Because Jesus paid for our diseases and sicknesses in His death, we have the power and His permission to lay hands on the sick and they shall recover or be healed. And if Satan happens to be the root cause, we are to cast him out using His name. "By His stripes we are healed" is the foundation for the healing of all sicknesses and diseases. His stripes are the proof or the receipt of our health and healing (cf. Isaiah 53:4-6).

Armed with this truth and the power of the Holy Spirit, no Christian can allow Satan to oppress, oppose or put to shame. Let me give you the example of the healing of the lame man at the gate of the temple called Beautiful. Peter said, "Silver and gold have I none; but such that I have give I thee: In the name of Jesus Christ of Nazareth rise up and walk." Peter later recounting the same incident said:

> **"And his name through faith in his name hath made this man strong, whom ye see and know: yea, the faith which is by him hath given him this perfect soundness in the presence of you all" (Acts 3:16).**

The miracle was by the 'faith of Jesus,' total belief in His victory over the ravages of sin. Peter had no victories of his own, except that which was earned for him by Jesus. Technically, when Jesus died, we died with Him and when He rose to life again, we rose together with Him. Now that He has ascended and is seated on the throne of glory, you and I are also seated together with Him in that heavenly place, which is far above all principalities and powers.

Jesus died in our place; we were crucified in Him: "He died for me," is the ground or the foundation on which we stand to win every battle in life. It is our authority to remove every mountain and break every yoke:

> **"But God, who is rich in mercy, for his great love wherewith he loved us, even when we were dead in sins, hath quickened us together with Christ, (by grace ye are saved;) And hath raised us up together, and made us sit together in heavenly places in Christ Jesus:**
>
> **That in the ages to come he might shew the exceeding riches of his grace in his kindness toward us through Christ Jesus. For by grace are ye saved through faith; and**

that not of yourselves: it is the gift of God: Not of works, lest any man should boast" (Ephesians 2:4-9).

Death has no control over Christians because each of us died to death in Christ. The life we now live or possess is the life given to us by God through His Son. Everyone born possesses immortality. For Christians, physical death is a blessing; it is the gateway to glory; it is an opportunity to enter into life; the opportunity to put on the new suit, which is reserved by God in Christ (1 Corinthians 15:50-53).

Living by the faith of Jesus is the only guarantee for victory under every kind of circumstance. You can never fail when you depend on the faith of the Son of God. Nothing can defeat the believer if he holds unto His faith. Remember, His faith is what He did for you, which includes His life, death, resurrection, ascension, and enthronement. He is the reason that Christians are seated in heavenly places. Those who through His faith keep the commandment of God can endure every trial:

"Here is the patience of the saints: here are they that keep the commandments of God, and the faith of Jesus" (Revelation 14:12).

We are not saved by His faith to believe in ourselves afterwards. Faith is not belief in abstract and senseless rituals and doctrines of fallen man and worship of demons. It is not an intelligent or unintelligent act of the mind. Faith does not contradict reason, rather it transcends:

"That your faith should not stand in the wisdom of men, but in the power of God" (1 Corinthians 2:5).

The ways of God transcends reasoning. Faith is required to appreciate God for all that He is, has done and will continue to do. No man can walk with God without faith. For example, the substitutionary death of the one man Jesus two thousand years ago, may not appeal to reason for many people, but it is overly appreciated and accepted where there is faith.

The most precious thing Adam and Eve lost in the fall was their Faith in God. They had intact mind, reason, conscience, etc., but none could bridge the broken relationship or restore their faith in God; it was lost forever. Faith in the Son of God is the only sure foundation for all virtues including love, reason, and conscience:

> "And beside this, giving all diligence, add to your faith virtue; and to virtue knowledge; and to knowledge temperance; and to temperance patience; and to patience godliness; and to godliness brotherly kindness; and to brotherly kindness charity.
>
> For if these things be in you, and abound, they make you that ye shall neither be barren nor unfruitful in the knowledge of our Lord Jesus Christ.
>
> But he that lacketh these things is blind, and cannot see afar off, and hath forgotten that he was purged from his old sins" (2 Peter 1:5-9).

Faith believes all that God says about His beloved Son Jesus Christ. True wisdom can only be found in God; it comes by the fear of God. Faith trembles and is eager to do God's will. Faith always obeys. Jesus is the wisdom of God; wisdom and knowledge are concentrated in Him. Education without faith in God produces arrogance and self-righteousness. Let us gain wisdom by following the example of Paul:

> "But what things were gain to me, those I counted loss for Christ. Yea doubtless, and I count all things but loss for the excellency of the knowledge of Christ Jesus my Lord: for whom I have suffered the loss of all things, and do count them but dung, that I may win Christ.
>
> And be found in him, not having mine own righteousness, which is of the law, but that which is through the faith of Christ, the righteousness which is of God by

faith: That I may know him, and the power of his resurrection, and the fellowship of his sufferings, being made conformable unto his death" (Philippians 3:7-10).

As far as Paul was concerned his one and only goal in life was to know Christ and to know Him experientially; nothing comes close to the exceeding privilege and value of knowing Christ. Standing in faith and living under the grace and mercy of God, each of us must strive to grow in the knowledge of Jesus Christ (2 Peter 3:18). To be more candid, it is a great privilege and an honor to be united with the only Son of God and to come to a perfect understanding of Him. No sacrifice and offering of any man can come close to what Jesus has done for mankind.

The pleasure of God is His Son; anyone who loves the Son is also loved by the Father. Anyone who hates the Son also hates the Father. God will only accept sinners who come to Him on the basis of what His Son has accomplished for them. If anybody wants to please God, he is required to have a deep seated faith in what God has already done through Christ; this is the one and only way. By Faith, we avail ourselves of the gifts of God, and submit ourselves in obedience to God's commands.

Very often, when we say we believe God to solve a particular problem for us, we are found at the same time busy devising other schemes to help ourselves solve it. Instead of waiting, we are found to be busy working to bail ourselves out. We seem to be always ahead of Him having no patience to wait for Him to tell us what to do or how to get out of the problem. This is one of the reasons we always find ourselves time and time again fighting the same problem with no ending in sight.

All the promises of God are ye and amen in Him, but each of us must believe His word or promise to benefit from them. Faith as a grain of mustard seed is all that is needed to remove a whole mountain and for it to be cast into the sea. Every Christian has received from God through the Gospel the measure of faith:

"For I say, through the grace given unto me, to every man
that is among you, not to think of himself more highly
than he ought to think; but to think soberly, according as
God hath dealt to every man the measure of faith" (Ro -
mans 12:3).

With God nothing is impossible, and because of your
union with Christ, nothing is impossible to you as well. You
can always tap into His supernatural ability through His
indwelling presence, to accomplish deeds for His glory. Where
there is true love, there is faith, and where there is faith, there
is genuine service. Faith without service is no faith, for faith
worketh by love. Faith works by obedience; unbelief works by
disobedience:

"If you love me keep my commandment" (John 14:15).

Love, faith, and obedience are inseparable under all
circumstances. Faith demonstrates itself in works, for faith
without works is dead. Genuine faith has one eye on His word and
the other on His service. God sent His Word to bless mankind;
anyone who has His Word in him is, therefore, an extension of
his blessings to other men. We pass on the love received to others.
His love is the standard for the love we must show unto others. If
He gave us all, then we must give all to Him.

Probably, the reason love for the brethren is so low among
Christians is because we have not understood the cost of our
redemption. For example, you can only forgive so much before
you know and understand how much you have been forgiven.
To drive home this point, I will like to use the parable as told
by Jesus:

"Then came Peter to him, and said, Lord, how oft shall
my brother sin against me, and I forgive him? till seven
times? Jesus saith unto him, I say not unto thee, Until
seven times: but, Until seventy times seven.

Therefore is the kingdom of heaven likened unto a certain king, which would take account of his servants. And when he had begun to reckon, one was brought unto him, which owed him ten thousand talents.

But forasmuch as he had not to pay, his lord commanded him to be sold, and his wife, and children, and all that he had, and payment to be made. The servant therefore fell down, and worshipped him, saying, Lord, have patience with me, and I will pay thee all. Then the lord of that servant was moved with compassion, and loosed him, and forgave him the debt.

But the same servant went out, and found one of his fellowservants, which owed him an hundred pence: and he laid hands on him, and took him by the throat, saying, Pay me that thou owest. And his fellowservant fell down at his feet, and besought him, saying, Have patience with me, and I will pay thee all. And he would not: but went and cast him into prison, till he should pay the debt.

So when his fellowservants saw what was done, they were very sorry, and came and told unto their lord all that was done. Then his lord, after that he had called him, said unto him, O thou wicked servant, I forgave thee all that debt, because thou desiredst me: Shouldest not thou also have had compassion on thy fellowservant, even as I had pity on thee?

And his lord was wroth, and delivered him to the tormentors, till he should pay all that was due unto him. So likewise shall my heavenly Father do also unto you, if ye from your hearts forgive not every one his brother their trespasses" (Mathew 18:21-35).

If only Christians can understand how poor they were before Christ made them rich by becoming poor for them, they might not hesitate to share whatever they have with the poor and needy of this world. Each of us must appreciate that whatever service we render to God or to fellow man is based upon a mature understanding of what Jesus has already done for us by grace.

When people perish, they perish because of the lack of the knowledge of the grace of God. For example, if you have experienced some comfort during the time of sickness and disease, then it is your turn to share the comfort you received with others who are now experiencing their own. This is the reason why preachers must be vested with the truth of God, so that they may be able to dispense it accurately for the salvation of mankind and render holy services to God:

> **"All scripture is given by inspiration of God, and is profitable for doctrine, for reproof, for correction, for instruction in righteousness: That the man of God may be perfect, thoroughly furnished unto all good works"** (2 Timothy 3:16-17).

In an age where everything is almost done on the fast lane, few Christians actually spend time to study the Bible thoroughly for themselves. Many rely solely on the information from their leaders or what they hear from their preachers. I am not saying this is bad, but it is important we check the validity of what is heard with the word of God. We live right when the word of God is received right. Every Christian must be a good student of the Bible:

> **"Study to shew thyself approved unto God, a workman that needeth not to be ashamed, rightly dividing the word of truth"** (2 Timothy 2: 15).

Faith is a winner, faith never fails: "For whatsoever is born of God overcometh the world: and this is the victory that overcometh the world, even our faith" (1 John 5:4). "Faith is being sure of what we hope for and certain of what we do not see. For example, by faith we understand that the universe was formed at God's command, so that what is seen was not made out of what was visible.

"By faith Abraham, when he was called to go to a place he would later receive as his inheritance, obeyed and went, even though he did not know where he was going. By faith Abraham, even though he was past age—and Sarah herself was barren—was enabled to become a father because he considered him faithful who had made the promise.

By faith Moses' parents hid him for three months after he was born, because they saw he was no ordinary child, and they were not afraid of the king's edict. By faith Moses, when he had grown up, refused to be known as the son of Pharaoh's daughter. He chose to be mistreated along with the people of God rather than to enjoy the pleasures of sin for a short time. He regarded disgrace for the sake of Christ as of greater value than the treasures of Egypt, because he was looking ahead to his reward.

By faith, the people passed through the Red Sea as on dry land; but when the Egyptians tried to do so, they were drowned. By faith the walls of Jericho fell, after the people had marched around them for seven days. Women received back their dead, raised to life again. Others were tortured and refused to be released, so that they might gain a better resurrection. Some faced jeers and flogging, while still others were chained and put in prison. They were stoned; they were sawed in two; they were put to death by the sword. They went about in sheepskins and goatskins, destitute, persecuted and mistreated— the world was not worthy of them. They wandered in deserts and mountains, and in caves and holes in the ground" (cf. Hebrews 11).

All the above people were commended for their faith, yet none of them received what had been promised. God had it all planned out in such a way that only together with us would they be made perfect. They are at the moment told to wait patiently for we who through the same faith would become victorious.

In conclusion, "Faith is the substance (assurance) of things hoped for, the evidence (conviction) of things not seen"

(Hebrews 11:1). The Spirit of God makes known in God's word certain things not seen, and produces within the Christian the convictions that these things actually exist. Without faith it is impossible to please God. He that cometh to God must believe that He is, and that He is the rewarder of them that diligently seek Him. Have faith in God, Amen (Mark 11:22).

Notes

Chapter Twelve

WORKING FROM FAITH

Saved by faith and kept by faith, Christians work from faith; true faith is always accompanied by good works. Goodness is greatness. This chapter answers the question about how transcended people make a living; how they execute the work of God. Whatever Christians do and say, they do out of faith or by faith. Faith is what produces works:

> "But wilt thou know, O vain man, that faith without works is dead?" (James 2:20).

Work originated with God who worked to give us the world in which we live. God worked for six days and rested on the seventh day:

> "And on the seventh day God ended his work which he had made; and he rested on the seventh day from all his work which he had made" (Genesis 2:2).

After He had created man, He instituted work for man. Man was not to be idle, but through faith, be a steward to the things that were created by faith and entrusted to him:

> "And God blessed them, and God said unto them, Be fruitful, and multiply, and replenish the earth, and sub-

due it: and have dominion over the fish of the sea, and over the fowl of the air, and over every living thing that moveth upon the earth" (Genesis 1:28).

Born of God, Christians are like their Father in many ways: "As He is, so are we in this world." How work is to be done on earth by man can be found by examining the first three verses of the book of Genesis:

"In the beginning God created the heaven and the earth. And the earth was without form, and void; and darkness was upon the face of the deep. And the Spirit of God moved upon the face of the waters. And God said, Let there be light: and there was light" (Genesis 1:1-3).

"In the beginning," means the absolute beginning of everything but God. In these three verses, we find how the triune God made all things. God introduces Himself as the one who existed and who began all things:

"I have made the earth, and created man upon it: I, even my hands, have stretched out the heavens, and all their host have I commanded" (Isaiah 45:12).

The Word is introduced as the means by which all things were made. The Holy Spirit is introduced as the executive power that brings that which is spoken into being. So on the divine side, we find work as being done by God, through the Word and by the Spirit.

In the same vein, on the human side, the work of God is done by man through the word of God and by the Holy Spirit. The All Powerful omnipotent God has the power to carry out whatever He wishes or wills (Jeremiah 32:17); to do requires no effort on His part. He is never weary nor tired (Isaiah 40:27); He operates unspent.

Christians too can do all things through the power of the Holy Spirit, and by trusting the Holy Spirit can accomplish all that is required of them. Everything God does is good, and Christians are called to be followers of that which is good:

"Be ye therefore followers of God as dear children" (Ephesians 5:1).

God instructed Moses to document for mankind how He made the universe, thus leaving humanity an example to follow. God worked from faith and by that, man must also work from faith. God simply called into being all that He had planned to do. The God of faith simply called things forth or commanded them to stand up and they were created:

"Let them praise the name of the LORD: for he commanded, and they were created" (Psalm 148:5).

For the purpose of clarity, I shall tackle these three phrases or divine persons separately and in relation to work.

God

From Genesis chapter 1:1-3, we first learn that even though God offers no explanation of Himself, He is very much aware of Himself and what He does. God is the source of all power; He is all powerful and all knowing. Unlimited in power, He works all things in conformity to His own will and purpose. He works all things for His own pleasure, and for His personal end. God created the whole universe for Himself; for His own delight, which is the person of Jesus Christ:

"For by Him all things were created that are in heaven and that are on earth, visible and invisible, whether thrones or dominions or principalities or powers. All things were created through Him and for Him" (Colossians 1:16).

Everything in God's creation is pleasurable, beautiful, ennobling, and enriching. Humans, animals and plants, the solar system were all created and exist for His pleasure:

"Thou art worthy, O Lord, to receive glory and honour and power: for thou hast created all things, and for thy pleasure they are and were created" (Revelation 4:11).

God is self-sufficient. All created beings depend on Him, but He Himself is unconscious of need. He is independent of all that He creates; He is self-subsisting within Himself:

"If I were hungry, I would not tell thee: for the world is mine, and the fulness thereof" (Psalm 50:12).

Because God created man for His pleasure, Christians share with God His pleasure. When we seek to do His will or do those things which are pleasing to Him, we have His approval to use his name for greater accomplishments (1 Thessalonians 4:1; Hebrews 11:5). Living, serving and working in faith is the only way and means to please God:

"But without faith it is impossible to please him: for he that cometh to God must believe that he is, and that he is a rewarder of them that diligently seek him" (Hebrews 11:6).

The duty of man from the beginning of his creation has been to have dominion over things created and to be fruitful. Man's work was cut out for him from the beginning by his creation:

"And God blessed them, and God said unto them, Be fruitful, and multiply, and replenish the earth, and subdue it: and have dominion over the fish of the sea, and over the fowl of the air, and over every living thing that moveth upon the earth" (Genesis 1:28).

 From the things made, man was permitted to make a living by depending on God for wisdom and knowledge and ability; to make a living on what God has said. Man cannot make things out of nothing, but he can work from that which God has made.

Everything changed for man when sin entered into him and into the world. Sin changed man and so with work as planned by God. Through sin, man abdicated his duty to God and his responsibility to nature. The indiscriminate destruction of nature by greedy man is no surprise. Man lost his faith in God through sin. In his fall, faith in God and His word was lost. Sin is a destroyer; it corrupts and mars everything that is beautiful; like leprosy, it deforms, maims, and kills everything in its path.

But, glory to God, this loss on the part of man is regained through Christ by new birth. Christians can resume the God-given responsibility; work as ordained by God can be done through faith. Christians can also live the God kind of life by depending on God for everything; for sustenance and preservation (1 Corinthians 1:29-30). Possessing the God kind of faith, Christians work from faith. Christians ought to work from faith:

"He that saith he abideth in Him ought himself also so to walk, even as He walked (1 John 2:6).

There are only two persons with whom all things are possible, God and the Christian (God and His children). Christians are heavenly royals and ambassadors on earth. Whatever they bind on earth is bound in heaven; meaning, we have the approval of heaven to promote the will of God on earth. As citizens of heaven, Christians are admonished to stay clear of all that defiles our nature and is foreign to the will of God. But, this is no mean task for the fleshly minded. It may cost us everything; all that may be dear to us:

"But what things were gain to me, those I counted loss for Christ. Yea doubtless, and I count all things but loss for the excellency of the knowledge of Christ Jesus my Lord: for whom I have suffered the loss of all things, and do count them but dung, that I may win Christ, And be found in him, not having mine own righteousness, which is of the law, but that which is through the faith of Christ, the righteousness which is of God by faith" (Philippians 3:7-9).

Because of sin, work as intended by God can only begin at new birth. Through faith, Christians can prosper in all that they set their hands on to do. Work for man is primarily doing the will of God:

"For God shall bring every work into judgment, with every secret thing, whether it be good, or whether it be evil" (Ecclesiastes 12:14).

Every human being is blessed by God. To every man is given the stewardship of the planet. The wealth of this earth is for all to share; every man has the right to share in the wealth of the earth. Poverty is violence against humanity; to be poor amid profusion is a form of torture and must be eradicated.

God is fully aware of Himself; therefore, Christians must also be fully aware of who they are in Christ and work from that position of knowledge. During the temptation of Jesus Christ, Satan demanded of Jesus to prove His relation to the Father: "if thou be the Son of God" (Mathew 4:3). At every point in our sojourn on earth, Satan, would want to know if indeed we trust every word that proceedeth from the mouth of the living God fully.

Satan will tempt each of us (even if he is not doing that already) to seek our own desires and glory. But, when we fulfill the desire of God, He will also take care of our wants:

"Delight thyself also in the LORD: and he shall give thee the desires of thine heart" (Psalm 37:4).

The desire of the righteous shall be granted (Proverbs 11:23). We must not take advantage of our new standing in God or as Christians for personal aggrandizement. In all our actions, we must be sure our motives are with clear conscience. Through faith, we can know God. God is greatly honored when a Christian walks in faith. Born the second time, the new man cannot walk in the flesh because we are not in the flesh. There is a reason why God placed the new man in the old body; "that the Excellency of the power may be of God and not of us" (2 Corinthians 4:7).

His Word

At each stage of the creation order, we read the phrase, God said, meaning, God spoke. He sent forth His word and they were created. The universe did not exist until God spoke the word. But, as God spoke, things outside Him began to emanate; for example, first there was the original mass, then light, dry land, the sun, moon, stars, etc. Only man was not created directly from the spoken word, but, even then, God spoke to begin the process of formation and finally the making: "And God said, Let us make man in our image, after our likeness" (Genesis 1:26).

Similarly, man must first speak the word of God into every situation for the will of God to be done. From His written word, Christians can command things made to change form, move, destroy strongholds and heal the sick and afflicted to the glory of the Lord: "Death and life are in the power of the tongue: and they that love it shall eat the fruit thereof" (Proverbs 18:21).

Man can make a living from the word of God because God said: "And God said, Behold, I have given you every herb bearing seed, which is upon the face of all the earth, and every tree, in which is the fruit of a tree yielding seed; to you it shall be for meat" (Genesis 1:29). We eat fruit, vegetables, and meat because God said that is our diet, other than that man would never have known.

Jesus was absolutely correct when He said: "man shall not live by bread alone, but by every word that proceedeth out of the mouth of God." The source of bread is more important than the bread itself; likewise, the source of life, more important than the life itself. Individual Christians have God's permission and authority to speak into existence His promises and will:

"Whereby are given unto us exceeding great and precious promises: that by these ye might be partakers of the divine nature, having escaped the corruption that is in the world through lust" (2 Peter 1:4).

Thy will be done on earth is the responsibility of every man. If only Christians can believe; if we take God at His word, nothing shall be impossible. God's word is always good and would always perform for us; His word would not return to Him void. His word would never run dry:

"So shall my word be that goeth forth out of my mouth: it shall not return unto me void, but it shall accomplish that which I please, and it shall prosper in the thing whereto I sent it" (Isaiah 55:11).

All the promises of God are as good as Himself; they cannot fail. Every Christian is called upon to make a living by the promises of God: "Having therefore these promises, dearly beloved, let us cleanse ourselves from all filthiness of the flesh and spirit, perfecting holiness in the fear of God" (2 Corinthians 7:1).

We cannot make a living out of dishonest gain and neither can we keep back the wages of those who work for us. But, we can make a descent living by trusting the word of the Living God. Then we shall be ready at all times to help those who seek our help:

"For all the promises of God in him are yea, and in him Amen, unto the glory of God by us" (2 Corinthians 1:20).

How each of us lives, depends on how much of God's word we are willing to trust. Each of us can only speak into existence that which is believed (of course, not everything we wish). Only the word of God has built-in power to perform or create. We repeat His word or say His word after Him by what we read and know.

It is rather unfortunate that many Christians are very selective when it comes to the Bible; holding the scissors of unbelief, we cut out all that is distasteful to us. We cut out until we finally conclude; I have no interest in that book.

Each day, each hour, we must speak out the promises of God. We must call forth the promises of God into our lives and situations; we must call His word into existence. Each of us can only go as far as we believe, for none of us can go beyond our belief:

"We having the same spirit of faith, according as it is written, I believed, and therefore have I spoken; we also believe, and therefore speak" (2 Corinthians 4:13).

Christians can only work from a position of total dependence and trust. Work for the Christians is doing the will of God. Obedience to the word of God is work. When you spend eight hours a day, five days a week reading and studying the word of God, it can be considered as working and surely God will pay you. If carnal man can employ us with just a promise on a piece of paper with his signature promising to pay us at the end of the month and we believe, how much more the infallible God:

"But he answered and said, It is written, Man shall not live by bread alone, but by every word that proceedeth out of the mouth of God" (Mathew 4:4).

Jesus was one day asked the question, "What shall we do, that we might work the works of God?" His response, to the amazement of His listeners was:

"This is the work of God, that ye believe on him whom he hath sent" (John 6:29; cf. verse 28).

Through faith, Christians like their heavenly Father, can call those "things which be not as though they were" (Romans 4:17); for we walk by faith, and not by sight. Living by the promises of God, Christians become partakers of the divine nature (2 Peter 1:4). God has made humanity stewards of His creation and Christians His co-laborers; if we do not activate His promises into our lives and that of our children, then very little will happen. We would be reduced to the common grace that is available to all mankind.

What is the use of positive words or thinking without the foundation of God's word? Believing in yourself, depending on yourself, working hard, studying the system, being positive in your thinking, etc., are not bad in themselves but to what profit is it to the believer without a solid belief in God's word or the solid foundation of truth as revealed in scripture: "Jesus died for all, that they which should live should not unto themselves, but unto Him which died for them, and rose again."

King Solomon summarized for us what life outside faith looks like: It is "Vanity and vexation of spirit" (Ecclesiastes 4:16); It is great sweat from the brow which ends in a pathetic death with no satisfaction in sight; with no reward and no hope for the future: "Let us hear the conclusion of the whole matter: Fear God, and keep His commandments: For this is the whole duty of man" (Ecclesiastes 12:13). Faith loves; faith obeys.

Faith believes and speaks out that which is believed. We do not just speak some positive words hoping that God would endorse our wishful thinking. If we learn to set our eyes on His holy word and speak it into action; if we command His promises to come forth, then we are guaranteed a good ride in the Spirit. We are guaranteed a transcended life of blissfulness here and hereafter.

Nothing happens if we say or do nothing. Jesus said; "whatsoever you shall bind on earth shall be bound in heaven and whatsoever you shall lose on earth shall be lose in heaven" (Mathew 18:18). Again, Jesus said: "For verily I say unto you, that whosoever shall say to this mountain be thou removed and be thou cast into the sea; and shall not doubt . . . he shall have whatsoever he saith" (Mark 11:23).

God has given us His precious promises; we can choose to believe or not choose to believe. However, we must remember without faith in His word, it is absolutely impossible to please Him. Every man has a choice in this life concerning the word of God; God has sent for His word to heal us, but each of must decide whether we want it or not. Likewise, man is free to choose to reject Christ; each of us is responsible for our actions or what we do and say.

No matter what may confront us in this life, we have a choice to use either the natural (our own ways and means) or the faith way (rely absolutely on the word or promises of God). For example, if your child is sick, you can use the drug provided by your doctor or the pharmacy or solely trust the word of God for the healing of your child:

> "He sent his word, and healed them, and delivered them from their destructions" (Psalm 120:20).

Some for fear of death depend on both methods. For this group, they believe that common sense must prevail, for we cannot afford to be so spiritually minded, that we become earthly foolish. Again, each of us can only live by what we believe; the choice is ours. We can memorize all the promises of God and inscribe them on every wall in our house or on our body, but, if we do not believe and speak them into existence, they would forever remain unfulfilled promises and what a dishonor that would be to you and to God that would be.

Let me give you another example from the experiences of the people of Israel. God sent forth His word to heal them from the sin of unbelief and it did not matter who:

> "And the people spake against God, and against Moses, Wherefore have ye brought us up out of Egypt to die in the wilderness? for there is no bread, neither is there any water; and our soul loatheth this light bread.
>
> And the LORD sent fiery serpents among the people, and they bit the people; and much people of Israel died.
>
> Therefore the people came to Moses, and said, We have sinned, for we have spoken against the LORD, and against thee; pray unto the LORD, that he take away the serpents from us. And Moses prayed for the people.
>
> And the LORD said unto Moses, Make thee a fiery serpent, and set it upon a pole: and it shall come to pass, that every one that is bitten, when he looketh upon it, shall live. And Moses made a serpent of brass, and put it upon a pole, and it came to pass, that if a serpent had bitten any man, when he beheld the serpent of brass, he lived" (Numbers 21:5-9).

The serpent of brass was for the healing of all; anyone who was bitten by a serpent. The healing was in the spoken word, if they obey they would be healed; if not, then each had himself to blame. It was up to each of them to do what they wanted to do with the word given by God and spoken to them by Moses. Further, I believe there were natural medicines for snake bites available. Everyone bitten by a snake could depend on the word of God and live, rely on the uncertainty of natural medicine, or do nothing and die.

All that a Christian may need must be spoken into existence. Each of us must repeat and command or speak the promises of God into our life and the life of our children. All that we need for life and godliness is already provided for by God. He is only waiting for each of us to speak them into action and to speak it into manifestation for His praise and glory. As joint heirs with Christ, the king of the universe has given us power and authority to use His name and His word for His glory. As we walk by faith and the world sees that there is a better and easy way to live, believe it or not, the world will begin to praise God, and some may even seek reconciliation with God:

"And believers were the more added to the Lord, multi-tudes both men and women" (Acts 5:14).

The world must see God in action from all we do. This is the way and the best way. God is the believer's supplier, and where there is a request, there is a supply; we have His word on that, "for all the promises of God in him are yea, and in him Amen, unto the glory of God by us. Where there is a need, there must be of a necessity, a calling forth and the necessity of supply. No matter what the need may be, for example: Job, marriage, children, money, peace, love for God, healing, we must first learn to call what we need into existence and this is the starting place for work in the life of each individual Christian. Some of us are prone to calling forth that which we don't want, instead of that which we want.

Ours are not positive words, we reiterate the promises of God; we speak His word: "For none of us liveth to himself or dieth to himself; whether we die or live, it is all for the Lord's glory: whether we live therefore, or die, we are the Lord's" (Romans 14:7-8). This method of calling forth transcends positive thinking. This way is beyond the natural. God has promised to supply the needs of every Christian, so Christians do not have to work for a living:

> "Therefore take no thought, saying, What shall we eat? or, What shall we drink? or, Wherewithal shall we be clothed? (For after all these things do the Gentiles seek:) for your heavenly Father knoweth that ye have need of all these things" (Mathew 6:31-32).

> "But my God shall supply all your needs according to his riches in glory by Christ Jesus" (Philippians 4:19).

> "Let your conversation be without covetousness; and be content with such things as ye have: for he hath said, I will never leave thee, nor forsake thee" (Hebrews 13:5).

Then, why do Christians work may be your question. The simple answer is that work for a Christian is an opportunity to share faith or belief. They work to reveal the will, the grace and mercy of God to a dying world. They live to work and share Christ; they are on earth for the king's business. The first employment of every Christian is an ambassador for Christ (servants of the Most High). They work so that they may be practically useful to all men. For example, if a Christian becomes rich, the purpose is to help the poor. Every Christian is set for life. In Christ, every Christian is rich. Ours is eternal life; ours is the resurrected life. As we have believed, so let us speak.

I pray that God may give to you the spirit of wisdom and revelation in the knowledge of Jesus Christ (Ephesians 1:7) and that we might be filled with the knowledge of His will in all wisdom and spiritual understanding (Colossians 1:9). May the Lord arm you with the knowledge of His will and grant great grace to accomplish His will, Amen.

The Spirit

God does not operate alone; He does not work in isolation and neither can we. Each time God spoke the Word, the Spirit manifested that which is said. God spoke the Word and the Spirit did the work and this is the formula for all divine activities: "For there are three that bear record in heaven, the Father, the Word, and the Holy Ghost: and these three are one" (1 John 5:7).

In the midst of darkness and chaos, the Spirit of God moved to prepare for the effectual creative Word of God: "And the Spirit of God moved upon the face of the waters" (Genesis 1:2). As God spoke the Word, the Spirit brought it into manifestation. As the will of God was expressed by the spoken Word, the Spirit brooding over the created mass of the earth executed that which was being said; the Spirit created order, beauty and time. The same Spirit also preserves that which is created.

Now, this is the Spirit that now dwells in each and every Christian. To every Christian is given the Spirit of God. Indwelling Spirit is the power of God to do the will of God: "For them that believe He gave them the power not only to live as sons of God, but work and live as sons of God." Jesus demonstrated this truth when He said the power of God is upon Him because He has been appointed: "to preach the Gospel to the poor, to heal the broken hearted, to preach deliverance to the captives, the recovering of sight to the blind, and to set at liberty them that are bruised.

In fact, God has not changed His method of working. He expects all His sons to work like Him. God takes over the ruined life of a sinner, speaks His Word concerning him and the Spirit works to brings out a saint; the creation of a saint is as stupendous as the creation of the heaven and earth. God brings new life out of the chaos of a sinful and perishing life.

Again, the Spirit's work does not stop after recreation, He preserves the saint. He continues the work of sanctification, and preservation of the saint unto the day of glorification. Jesus said: "My Father worketh hitherto, and I work" (John 5:17). God has given us His Spirit to do the work of the ministry.

As children of God, we speak into existence our Father's words and the Spirit executes that which we speak just as He did in the life of Jesus and in the creation of the earth. The Holy Spirit delights to honor His God's word as we speak them. Every word of God is the word of the Spirit and the word of Jesus Christ.

Christians must learn the ways of God. How glorious that would be and a change we can bring to the world, when our will is aligned with God's will and our answers have a 100% guarantee. The Holy God does not honor the request of men. He only honors the inspired word; words which are given by intuition, prophesy and words spoken from the Scriptures. The Spirit plays by the book because God cannot contradict Himself: "As He not said, and would He not do it?

Whatever a man may in life outside the will of God will in the end amounts to nothing; likewise, any request outside the will of God may not be granted. Be assured, God would not honor requests that are to gratify the flesh or propensities. He takes no delight in sensualities and the destruction of the soul. Only God knows what is good for us because He designed and made us. Joy, peace and prosperity is the portion of all those who do His will:

"Beloved, I wish above all things that thou mayest prosper and be in health, even as thy soul prospereth" Amen (3 John 2).

Good works

Every Christian is born again to do good works; we are saved unto good works. Good works is what man was originally created to do, and now believers are called upon to exercise the same. Good works cannot save anybody, but everybody that is saved must engage in good works. Jesus sent His Holy Spirit to make us good and to do good works through us. Even though Jesus is in heaven He is still going about doing the same good works He used to do while on earth through Christians (cf. Acts 10:38):

> **"For we are his workmanship, created in Christ Jesus unto good works, which God hath before ordained that we should walk in them" (Ephesians 2:10).**

Because of sin, man became corrupt and every works of his hands also became corrupt. But, Jesus "gave himself for us, that he might redeem us from all iniquity, and purify unto himself a peculiar people, zealous of good works" (Titus 2:14). He made us good that we might be engaged in honorable occupations. One must be made good to do good works. An unregenerate man cannot do good works as expected of God; he can do works that to men may be regarded as good works but before God they may be as filthy rags:

> **"The fool hath said in his heart, there is no God. They are corrupt, they have done abominable works, there is none that doeth good" (Psalm 14:1).**

> **"They profess that they know God; but in works they deny him, being abominable, and disobedient, and unto every good work reprobate" (Titus 1:16).**

God saved us and gave us the bible so that man may be equipped, thoroughly furnished unto all good works (2 Timothy 3:16,17). God desires that every Christian should be zealous for good works; be rich in good deeds, ready to distribute, and willing to communicate (1 Timothy 6:18). Christians are to show themselves a pattern of good works in a world which is full of darkness and wickedness. We must maintain good works by considering one another, to provoke unto love and to do good works (Hebrews 10:24).

A Christian who engages in good deeds is wise: "Who is a wise man and endued with knowledge among you? let him shew out of a good conversation his works with meekness of wisdom" (James 3:13):

> "But the wisdom that is from above is first pure, then peaceable, gentle, and easy to be intreated, full of mercy and good fruits, without partiality, and without hypocrisy" (James 3:17).

The words and works of a Christian are both a testimony of his faith in God. Jesus said God is glorified when we do good works:

> "Let your light so shine before men, that they may see your good works, and glorify your Father which is in heaven his witness of Christ" (Mathew 5:16).

—————————————

> "Having your conversation honest among the Gentiles: that, whereas they speak against you as evildoers, they may by your good works, which they shall behold, glorify God in the day of visitation" (1 Peter 2:12).

Good works have great recompense; they produce great reward: "Knowing that whatsoever good thing any man doeth, the same shall he receive of the Lord, whether he be bond or free" (Ephesians 6:8):

> "For other foundation can no man lay than that is laid, which is Jesus Christ. Now if any man build upon this foundation gold, silver, precious stones, wood, hay, stubble; every man's work shall be made manifest: for the day shall declare it, because it shall be revealed by fire; and

the fire shall try every man's work of what sort it is.

If any man's work abide which he hath built thereupon, he shall receive a reward. If any man's work shall be burned, he shall suffer loss: but he himself shall be saved; yet so as by fire" (1 Corinthians 3:11-13).

Every man's work shall be weighed against the price paid for salvation. Quality, which is the motive of our actions, shall be determined by Christ Jesus or the work of Christ. All who are saved will go to heaven, but not all who will go to heaven will receive a reward (John 5:24; 2 Corinthians 5:10). The possibility of losing the reward must be the concern of every Christian.

In conclusion, Christians work through the Christ Jesus (written word) and by the Holy Spirit in the same way God works through His Word and by His Spirit. In the beginning of creation, God made ready everything before man was made. Man woke up on the morning of his creation, an adult man with his food on the table, clothes in the closet, animals for sport, and transportation and a palace that contained all his children.

Likewise, God sent Jesus to prepare all that the new man would need before man could be born again. His righteousness, justification, sanctification, glorification, and natural and material needs are ready for him. Every Christian cannot but be good; be rich in good works. The measure we measure unto others, it shall be measured unto us; the good deeds we do unto others, same shall be done unto us: "For he shall have judgment without mercy, that hath shewed no mercy; and mercy rejoiceth against judgment" (James 2:13). A good deed is greatness. "Now unto our God and Father be the Glory throughout the ages. Amen.

Chapter Thirteen

WRITE YOUR OWN CHAPTER

Share the experience gained by reading this book with others, any one who may read this book after you. I have shared with you what God has shared with me, now it is your turn to share.

_____

_____

_____

_____

_____

_____

_____

_____

_____

_____

_____

_____

This is the beauty of Christianity: Diversity in unity

One Body
One God
One Faith
One Lord, Jesus Christ
One Baptism
Born by the Holy Spirit
Indwelt by the Holy Spirit
Led by the Holy Spirit
Gifted by the Holy Spirit
Possess fruit of the Holy Spirit
    Exercise the gifts of the Holy Spirit
        One Hope of Calling

Additional copies of this book and other titles
From Joseph DeGraft-Amanfu
Are available at your local bookstore and our website.

To contact
Visit our website at:

www.preachthegospel2all.com

The grace of our Lord Jesus Christ be with you all, Amen.

CPSIA information can be obtained at www.ICGtesting.com
Printed in the USA
BVOW05s1007110715

407853BV00004B/6/P